Church Undivided

Exploring God's Vision for Unity in 1 Corinthians 8–10

Bob Ingle

Sermon To Book
www.sermontobook.com

Church Undivided / Bob Ingle
ISBN-13: 978-1-945793-95-0

Unity. Such a simple word, yet one with profound implications for all organizations, especially the church. My forty years as senior minister at Southeast Christian Church taught me the critical importance of unity, and now Bob Ingle has written an excellent book detailing how you can create a spirit of unity in your church by applying biblical principles to your leadership. This book is easy to read, exceptionally practical, and profound in its application.
Bob Russell
Retired Senior Minister, Southeast Christian Church

If there is anything the church of Jesus Christ needs today, it is unity. As our nation falls further away from God as a result of politics, crime, racism, and rampant sinfulness, now is the ideal time for Jesus' bride to be light in a dark world and salt in a low-sodium society. Bob Ingle's *Church Undivided* can help the local church unite and become a major force in attacking the darkness in our world. This book will bless you and help unify your congregation to make a difference in our sin-sick world.
Fred Luter Jr.
Senior Pastor, Franklin Avenue Baptist Church, New Orleans, LA
Former President, Southern Baptist Convention

As a church leadership consultant, the topic of unity is a constant challenge. Using the wisdom and teachings of 1 Corinthians, Bob takes a strong and insightful look at how Paul's teachings to the Corinthians can be understood and applied in today's contexts. With helpful discussion questions at the end of each chapter, *Church Undivided* is a powerful tool for any leader working to build unity in their team.
Kadi Cole
Leadership Consultant, Executive Coach, and Author of ***Developing Female Leaders*** **(www.kadicole.com)**

Though saddled by division, confusion, and carnality, the church at Corinth is remarkably instructive for twenty-first century believers. Through the apostle Paul's Corinthian correspondence to an unhealthy, divided church, we learn how a healthy church is to look and function. I'm thankful for Bob Ingle bringing this message to bear from 1 Corinthians 8–10 in *Church Undivided.* All who care about church health and church unity will find this book a helpful resource.
Jason K. Allen, Ph.D.
President, Midwestern Baptist Theological Seminary, Kansas City, MO

Bob Ingle's exposé of the importance and need for unity in the local church is nothing short of brilliant. His treatment of how God intends His people to deal with personal liberties is a must-read not only for every pastor but for every Christ-follower. This book draws the curtain back on what I believe has been the "secret" of growth in every church Ingle has pastored: the why and how of doing church together as a spiritual family, willing to sacrifice rights for the sake of love. Well done, Bob Ingle!
David M. McAlpin, Ph.D.
Associate Professor of Biblical Interpretation
Midwestern Baptist Theological Seminary, Kansas City, MO

In my estimation, few topics are as neglected and misunderstood as that of church unity. In *Church Undivided*, Bob Ingle does not address church unity with a bent of liberalism that calls for unity with no structure or with an overly structured view that calls for uniformity and sameness. Rather, he takes us on a straightforward, practical journey through Scripture, showing how every Christian has a personal responsibility to defeat division and promote unity within God's family. I pray this book will become a treasure to the Church of Jesus Christ!
Pastor Chadd Pendergraft
Senior Pastor, Crescent Valley Baptist Church, Tahlequah, OK

This book is dedicated to my dad, who taught me in word and deed how to love and lead the church of Jesus Christ.

CONTENTS

CONTENTS

INTRODUCTION

Peace Makers, Takers, or Fakers?

You're dealing with some conflict in your church, right? How do I know that? Because conflict happens wherever two or more people are gathered. Just ask Adam and Eve, Paul and Barnabas, or Jesus and Judas. Being a Christ-follower does not make you immune to conflict. Some Christians have become disillusioned because they have assumed that, of all the people on earth, those who belong to the church should be able to maintain continual peace and endless harmony. While this is true in theory, it is certainly not true in practice.

The New Testament provides a plethora of evidence for the fact that every church should expect some level of conflict among its members. Where differences are possible, conflict is inevitable. And when iron sharpens iron, sparks always fly.

Leading a church through conflict, however, can be even more challenging than the conflict itself. Vance Havner humorously observed that a modern-day pastor should possess "the mind of a scholar, the heart of a child, and the hide of a rhinoceros."[1] My own father, a faithful shepherd for more than forty years, warned me early in my ministry: "Bob, an important part of being a pastor is to have a soft heart and thick skin. It's when you get those reversed that the whole church is in trouble." The Holy Spirit has reminded me of those wise words many times.

Take a moment to look around you. Generational division is undeniable. Racial tension is palpable. Marital breakdowns are continual. And most concerning, spiritual harmony seems impossible. Church fights are common, and church splits are expected. Best friends become strangers, brothers and sisters become enemies, and others around them become indifferent.

God's Way Forward

That is why, in our culture today, a unified church is one of the strongest evidences of the power of God and the truth of the gospel. In our increasingly fragmented world, a group of diverse believers who patiently work together, humbly serve one another, selflessly submit to each other, and lovingly stick together in good times and bad stands out starkly in the community.

God's Word has not changed. Unity in the local church remains a core essential that is to be developed, strengthened, and protected by every single Christ-follower. There are no exclusions, and no number of excuses will get us off the hook. Unity is a matter of spiritual life or death.

Dr. Sinclair Ferguson was right on target with these soul-stirring words: "The gospel is a message of reconciliation and peace with God. How can non-Christians be convinced that Christ reconciles us to God if we are not reconciled to each other?"[2]

In leading churches through change and conflict for nearly three decades, I have developed a passion for helping Christ-followers discern biblically what they simply enjoy when it comes to their church and what God absolutely commands. This has not always been easy for me or comfortable for them. It is here, however, that I've found some of the greatest traction in leading through turbulent conflict and coming out on the other side stronger, healthier, and wiser.

We all have preferences and opinions about what a church should be and do. Most of them are good and reasonable, but personal thoughts and desires are always secondary to the mandates and instructions given to us in God's inspired Word. This book will focus on developing the ability to discern between the two and helping church members to understand genuinely and follow humbly.

Corinth and the Struggle for Unity

One of the most divided churches we know of in the first century was the church in Corinth. You may be familiar with a set of letters Paul wrote to this church in response to their pleas for spiritual help. These letters constitute the books of 1 and 2 Corinthians.

These books offer divinely given insight about the nature of genuine godly behavior, worship that pleases the heart of God, attitudes that reflect our Savior, and informative details concerning Paul's unprecedented gospel ministry. Some of the most applicable material for churches today deals with how to view and work through inevitable disagreement and conflict.

Corinth: The City of Sinners

To grasp the full meaning of the letters Paul wrote, we must understand the city in which the Corinthians lived. First-century Corinth, having two seaports, was a major trade center in the Roman Empire. Ships from the east (Asia Minor, Syria, Phoenicia, and Egypt) and the west (Italy and Spain) came with their various cargoes to sell and trade. This flooded the city not only with mass merchandise, but also with thousands of foreign sailors, who needed housing and entertainment.

Corinth was also internationally known for the Isthmian Games, the second-largest athletic event in the world at the time. Contestants and spectators from all over the world came to be a part of this Olympics-type competition.

Additionally, lining the streets of the giant city of Corinth were massive temples devoted to the worship of cultic gods and goddesses like Aphrodite, Poseidon, Apollo, Hermes, and others. These temples occupied a prime position in society, serving social and economic functions in addition to religious ones.[3]

As commerce increased, tourism expanded, and the population exploded, Corinth gained the dubious reputation of being one of the most decadent and sexually indulgent cities of the entire ancient world. The city's moral corruption was so notorious that the term "Corinthianized" was used to describe those engulfed in flagrant sexual immorality.[4]

Now, guess what kind of people made up the fledgling congregation known as the church of Corinth. The members of the church were men and women who had once fully participated in all the debauchery the city had to offer. Paul reminded them of this fact:

> *Do you not know that the unrighteous will not inherit the kingdom of God? Do not be deceived. Neither fornicators, nor idolaters, nor adulterers, nor homosexuals, nor sodomites, nor thieves, nor covetous, nor drunkards, nor revilers, nor extortioners will inherit the kingdom of God.* ***And such were some of you.*** *But you were washed, but you were sanctified, but you were justified in the name of the Lord Jesus and by the Spirit of our God.*
>
> ***—1 Corinthians 6:9–11*** ***(NKJV, emphasis added)***

The Corinthians themselves were a master example of

the power of the gospel through which God saves, forgives, and changes people. They were no longer defined by their past, but by the Person of Jesus Christ.

Unfortunately, over time, the Corinthians had slid back into their old ways of life and old patterns of sin. Their eyes were blinded, and their hearts became calloused. Sin tasted good while grace had lost its flavor. The Corinthian church had become fraught with alcohol problems, lawsuits, power struggles, sexual immorality, divorce, apathy toward sin, disputes over worship, and crippling division.

God had brought the Corinthians out of the world, but they brought much of the world back into the church. Their conduct did not reflect their calling. Paul wrote to shine light on their offenses and lead them back to the path of joyful delight in the power of the gospel.

The Gospel: The Solution for Sinners

Before we go any further, we must clearly define what the gospel of Jesus Christ is. The gospel is the good news that Jesus Christ perfectly fulfilled God's law, died sacrificially for our sins, and physically rose from the dead to reconcile His people permanently to a holy God through repentance of sin and faith in Him.

When spiritually lost people believe the gospel, they are saved *from* something and *to* Someone. They are saved from suffering the penalty for their sin, which is eternal separation from God, and they are saved to the Person of Jesus Christ, who is eternal life. Those who were once dead in their sin are now alive in Christ. Saved people are set free and set apart to be God's ambassadors of grace, hope, and love.

The Result: The Salvation and Sanctification of Sinners

It is this glorious truth, in fact, that led Paul to begin

his corrective letter to the Corinthian Christians: "To the *church* of God in Corinth, to those *sanctified* in Christ Jesus and called to be his holy people..." (1 Corinthians 1:2, emphasis added).

The word *church* in Greek is *ekklesia*, which means "to be called out."[5] The church is made up of the "called out" ones. Christians are called out of the world, called out of sin, and called out of death. They are called out to be God's holy people among the unsaved sinners, whom they used to resemble.

Not only had the Corinthians been called out, but they also had been set apart. That's the meaning of *sanctified.* They weren't set apart as a special possession of God because of what they had done or not done, but because of what the Son of God had done for them and in them through His sinless life, sacrificial death, and triumphant resurrection.

Their transformation was so startling and undeniable that the whole city of Corinth would likely have taken notice. They were to Corinth what a single lit match is to a pitch-black cave. Why? Because "the light shines in the darkness, and the darkness has not overcome it" (John 1:5).

The Church: The Struggling Saints

Unfortunately, though the soul of the city was still pitch-black, the church wasn't shining all that bright. As relatively young Christ-followers, these Corinthians were failing to demonstrate the set-apart nature of the Christian life. Paul confessed that he had to address them as though they "belonged to this world" (1 Corinthians 3:1 NLT).

The called-out Corinthians appeared to go back where they came from in many ways. Their behavior reflected the culture around them rather than Christ within them. Practices like sexual immorality, drunkenness, favoritism, worship wars, and prideful arrogance still existed within their faith community. The Corinthians were failing in their attempts to separate themselves from the people they had once been.

Could this be the root issue of our evangelism problem in the American church today? Could it be that our message isn't being heard or believed because the world sees no difference between our lives and theirs? Could it be that the world really is looking for something different from what they have, but they don't see anything different in us? If we want them to believe in our Redeemer, shouldn't the church look and live a little more redeemed?

Paul: The Sandpaper Apostle

The Corinthians wrote a letter to Paul chronicling their ongoing sin issues and the relationship struggles deeply embedded within their church. Much of Paul's response had an exasperated tone. His words acted like sandpaper, scraping away at the ignorance and arrogance of these spiritual children he adored:

> *Brothers and sisters, I could not address you as people who live by the Spirit but as people who are still worldly—mere infants in Christ. I gave you milk, not solid food, for you were not yet ready for it. Indeed, you are still not ready. You are still worldly.*
>
> ***—1 Corinthians 3:1–3a** **(emphasis added)***

By this time, the Corinthians had been saved for nearly five years.[6] Paul didn't doubt the sincerity of their belief; he chided the deficiency of their growth. He wasn't complaining that they used to be immature babes in Christ; he was upset that they remained that way.

Babies are a blessing at the beginning, but it would be

awful if they stayed that way. Changing a baby's diaper is fine at the beginning of his or her life. But if you're still doing it a decade later due to your child's unwillingness to grow up, you might have a problem with that.

Paul said, in a sense: "After all this time, you still eat baby food and act in baby ways. You need to grow up!" Does their behavior remind you of the American church? It should. We have churches full of believers who show up but won't grow up. This produces fifty-year-old churches that don't act fifty, right? They never get past the basics. They never get out of the shallow end. They never move from what *they* want to what *God* wants. Their selfishness never turns to selflessness. They don't grow up; they just pass away.

Predictably, the next generation fills their shoes, follows their example, and lives the same way. The younger generation has been taught that those in the church who fight harder, shout louder, and stomp heavier will probably get their way.

This cycle was forming in the church of Corinth. However, Paul, fueled by the Spirit of truth, was determined to bring that cycle to a screeching halt.

The Choice: Steak or Veggie?

Among their many disputes, one specific disagreement split this church into two opposing groups. One group determined that it was a sin to eat meat sacrificed to idols in the pagan temples while the other group claimed that their gospel freedom permitted them to eat the meat without guilt (1 Corinthians 8). Without having any clear, direct biblical mandate one way or the other, neither side would budge for the sake of the other. Dissension deteriorated into dysfunction.

Remarkably, similar types of divisions can be seen in modern-day churches—perhaps not regarding the eating of meat, but concerning such issues as appropriate clothing, worship songs and styles, Bible translations, home schooling, and political party affiliation. These issues, and many others, can become divisive enough to split congregations or birth new denominations. Let's be honest here. What has our deep division over such issues truly solved? Are we sincerely pursuing biblical truth or simply clinging to our personal preferences?

Ultimately, 1 Corinthians teaches us that the resolution of our differences must be soaked in and overflowing with the grace and love that come from God alone. Lest we think that Paul's inspired words are not pertinent to the church today, let us remember that God's Word is relevant and consistent yesterday, today, and forever (Hebrews 13:8).

For more than twenty-five years, I have led growing, vibrant, mission-focused churches that have refused to hide within their holy huddles, hoping that Jesus will return soon and rescue them from the wicked sinners of this world. Instead, they have heard Jesus' clear command and accepted His great commission to go into all the world, making disciples who know, love, and serve Him (Matthew 28:18–20).

Along the way, I have learned that if we do not go together, we will most likely not go at all. Satan knows this all too well, so he applies constant pressure to the tensions and differences that threaten to split us up and tear us down. The first step toward church destruction is disconnection between its members.

For this reason, unity has become one of the most common topics on which I preach. In the last ten years, I have taught specifically on this subject dozens of times. In this brutally fragmented world, I'm convinced that unity cannot be taught too much or emphasized too often.

This book is born out of a year-long sermon series covering the entire book of 1 Corinthians. One section, chapters 8–10, created more conversation and required more instruction than any other. Reactions were quite varied. A few families left the church because they deemed my views on debatable issues too lenient and liberal. Others wept with relief as they experienced freedom from the shackles of legalism and immaturity.

These timely sermons gave our people a fresh perspective on sensitive issues they had avoided in the past and a desire to discuss them honestly with other believers. It is my hope that this book will do the same for you.

Where We Are Headed

Over the next several chapters, we will deep dive into this section of 1 Corinthians, with each chapter looking at unity from a different angle. We will look at the decision every believer must make when disagreements arise (Chapter One) as well as a new way to view our "rights" and preferences in light of the gospel (Chapter Two).

We will also diagnose two of the most common quandaries that arise in regard to church unity (Chapters Three and Four), and we will learn from Paul's powerful example of self-sacrifice (Chapter Five). In Chapters Six and Seven, we will learn not only of the cost of unity, but also of the passion required to stay the course. Finally, we will take delight in the ultimate motive and power for unity, which is the glory of God through the grace of Jesus Christ.

At the end of each chapter, a workbook section will guide you in your pursuit of gospel clarity and church unity. You can make use of this tool in your individual study or in a small-group format.

Church Undivided

As we study Scripture together, I pray that you will be

both encouraged and challenged to examine your understanding of the gospel, your love for Christ's church, your heart for people, your personal theological gray areas that limit spiritual growth, and your willingness to live selflessly and sacrificially for the cause of Christ in all areas of your life.

You may come to realize that you have been a "peace-faker" or a "peace-taker" in conflict rather than the peacemaker God called you to be. Remember that failure isn't final unless you're unwilling to change. Before we launch, take a moment to drink in these refreshing words from author and scholar Paul Tripp:[7]

> The church can and should be a motley group of believers working together for the gospel, but this kind of unity is counterintuitive to sinners. It requires love, patience and self-control—all character qualities we don't naturally have.
>
> If you and I ever want to experience true unity with one another, we need to take advantage of the abundant grace in Christ so that we can give that same grace to our brothers and sisters. And because of the Cross, that grace is made available to you every morning.

Let's taste some grace and learn how to be a church undivided.

CHAPTER ONE

The Choice: Fight or Unite

> *I appeal to you, brothers and sisters, in the name of our Lord Jesus Christ, that all of you agree with one another in what you say and that there be* ***no divisions*** *among you, but that you* ***be perfectly united*** *in mind and thought.*
>
> ***—1 Corinthians 1:10*** ***(emphasis added)***

> The church is not a museum for pristine saints, but a hospital ward for broken sinners.[8]
>
> **—Timothy Keller**

Something unusual happened at the Passion Play in the Ozarks years ago.[9] As the local man playing the part of Jesus carried the cross through the streets, he was hounded by a heckler on the sidelines. The actor became so irritated that he dropped the cross, stormed over to the heckler, and punched him out.

The director of the play, of course, was aghast. He took the actor aside and said, "Listen, you're playing the role of Jesus Christ, and He never retaliated. Even though someone may taunt you, you can't lose your cool. It destroys the image of Jesus we're trying to project."

The next night, the same heckler was back, hurling similar barbs at the man playing Jesus while he was carrying the cross. Once again, the actor couldn't handle it. He dropped the cross, stormed the crowd, and had to be restrained. Once again, the director took him aside and said, "If you don't control yourself, you're not going to keep your part as Jesus in this play!"

Well, the next night as the actor carried his cross through the streets, the same man was there, verbally jabbing him from the sidelines. But this time, the actor gritted his teeth, looked over at the heckler, and said, "I'll meet you after the resurrection."

That story could serve as a caricature of the church today. No doubt the bride of Christ has countless beautiful features, but those often go unseen because people can't take their eyes off of the glaring ugliness of our disputes and disharmony. We sing of our life in Christ on Sunday but live in the death of division all week long.

The vast majority of denominations are birthed not from new conviction, but from old conflict. In any spat between believers, the devil doesn't pick a side; he simply provides ammunition for all. His goal is to make sure no one runs out of bullets.

But let's not resign ourselves to believing that the church will always be what she's always been. Paul's words should remind us that we still have a choice in the matter. We can choose to fight or unite.

Overlooking Unity

I admit that *unity* is one of those words that people hear a lot but don't find particularly exciting. It's more likely to cause yawning than yearning for most, probably because unity is significantly more satisfying when it's experienced than when it's explained.

It's kind of like the word *kiss*. Have you ever read

William Whitney's definition of a kiss in *The Century Dictionary*? According to Whitney, a kiss is "a compression of the closed cavity of the mouth with a slight sound made when the contact of lips by two people is broken."[10] Say what? This definition makes you question Mr. Whitney's kissing history!

The truth is that if you've ever shared a kiss with someone, you know that the experience is much better than the explanation. Church unity is the same way. You will never understand the breathtaking beauty of it or the extreme need for it until you've either experienced unity or suffered a total lack of it within a local church setting.

Many of you can identify with the father who heard an awful ruckus coming from the backyard, where his daughter and some of her friends were playing. There was a lot of shouting and fussing, and it got rather heated at times. The dad decided to intervene. He called out from the back door, "Hey, what's going on? Stop all that fighting!" The daughter answered, "Oh, Daddy, we're not fighting. We're just playing church."

If the church doesn't become more interested in sticking together, she will continue to have a reputation for her members tearing each other apart.

Unity in the Corinthian Church

As they were imploding as a church, Paul pleaded with the Corinthians to give their attention to the restoration of harmony and peace:

> *I appeal to you, brothers and sisters, in the name of our Lord Jesus Christ, that all of you agree with one another in what you say and that there be no divisions among you, but that you be perfectly united in mind and thought.*
>
> ***—1 Corinthians 1:10***

Paul made a passionate plea to this body of believers because he understood that unity is mandatory for a church to be used mightily. You might remember that the Corinthian church was full of radically redeemed, extraordinarily gifted believers. Paul said that they did "not lack any spiritual gift" (1 Corinthians 1:7). When it came to serving God, they were qualified and capable of doing it all.

Yet, even though they had been miraculously rescued from hell by God's grace and tremendously gifted to serve Christ with their lives, over time they became less and less enamored with God's grace and more and more consumed with their own desires. Selfishness and sinfulness caused major rifts and divisions among them.

The apostle Paul, their former pastor, wrote them this strong, emotional letter of love, rebuke, and correction. In the first nine verses, he greeted them with his love (1 Corinthians 1:1–3), reassured them of their salvation (1 Corinthians 1:8), and reminded them of God's amazing grace (1 Corinthians 1:9).

Then, from verse 10 to the end of the chapter, Paul launched into the corrective part of his letter to the church in Corinth. At that time, the Corinthian church had some major problems: people getting drunk at church functions, dysfunctional families falling apart, marriages ending in divorce, spiritual gifts being abused, lawsuits aimed at fellow church members, sexual immorality running rampant. Looking at their laundry list of shortcomings, I can't help but think of Kevin DeYoung's quip, "The next time someone tells you, 'The Church is full of a bunch of hypocrites,' you can respond, 'You don't know the half of it.'"[11]

However, Paul didn't start the letter by mentioning any of these sinful subjects. He knew that these issues were not the Corinthians' biggest problem. There was something even more pressing, more damaging, and more dangerous than all the others: *division* and *dissension*.

Quarreling and conflict caused a lack of unity within the body. A divided body always leads to deadly results. Paul knew that if the problem of disunity was not dealt with, the other problems wouldn't matter because the church would cease to exist.

Unity in the Church Today

Undoubtably, this same problem threatens the spiritual health and community impact of most churches in America. We must understand that unity is mandatory, not optional, for *every* church. It is non-negotiable.

One of my favorite pastors, D. Martyn Lloyd-Jones, certainly believed this to be true. He wrote the following words:[12]

> Our first and chief concern as Christians should be to guard and to preserve this precious, wondrous unity of the Spirit. ... If we believe in God, we must ever feel that our first duty is to guard this unity, to preserve it at all costs, to strain every nerve and be diligent in endeavoring to keep it and manifest it.

No wonder Paul wanted to deal with the conflicts among the Corinthians first. First Corinthians 1:11 states, "...there are contentions among you" (NKJV). Contentions are quarrels. Unresolved quarrels lead to ongoing conflict. Ongoing conflict is like life-threatening cancer. Paul recognized that the contentions among the Corinthians were siphoning the power of God within the church and stealing the church's influence in the surrounding community.

Church unity is a central component of our ability to evangelize our community. Just as children of parents who are constantly fighting have a hard time believing in marriage, people who witness disunity in the church have a hard time believing in the gospel message we preach. Severed relationships within our church negatively affect our ability to communicate with those outside of our church who are watching our lives as well as listening to our words.

Chuck Colson was right when he wrote:[13]

> The world isn't looking at our tracts and rallies and telecasts and study manuals. It is looking at us and how we behave. When it fails to see the unity of Jesus' followers—the church—it fails to see the validation that Christ is indeed the Son of the living God.

I couldn't agree more. A selfless Christ will never be seen through selfish Christians, and a unifying gospel will not be conveyed through a divided people.

The Importance of Unity

In Ephesians 4:1, Paul made the following earnest plea to the church: "live a life worthy of the calling you have received." In other words, make sure that your walk matches what you say you believe. You claim that God called you to be His own. Prove it by living accordingly.

In the verses that immediately follow, notice Paul's primary mandate to those wanting to demonstrate that they have been authentically called by Christ:

> ***Make every effort to keep the unity of the Spirit through the bond of peace.*** *There is one body [the church] and one Spirit [the Holy Spirit], just as you were called to one hope [the return of Christ] when you were called; one Lord [Jesus], one faith [the gospel of Jesus Christ], one baptism [of the Holy Spirit into Christ]; one*

> *God and Father of all, who is over all and through all and in all.*
>
> **—*Ephesians 4:3–6*** *(emphasis and comments added)*

Clearly, Paul believed that unity with God's family was evidence of a person's calling into His family.

Similarly, on the eve of Jesus' death, the unity of His church was on His heart. Gathered with His disciples, He prayed the following words:

> *...I pray also for those who will believe in me through their message, that all of them may be* ***one****, Father, just as you are in me and I am in you. May they also be in us so that* ***the world may believe that you have sent me****.*
>
> **—*John 17:20–21*** *(emphasis added)*

Did you see that? Church unity strengthens gospel clarity. Unity gives believers a more *detailed* picture of the gospel and the world a more *accurate* picture of the gospel. Forgiven people reflect the character of their forgiving God to an exponentially greater degree when they commit to following Christ together, no matter the cost.

The Ingredients of Unity

It does us no good to understand our dire need for unity if we have no clue about the components that form it. Biblically, what are the essential ingredients for authentic unity in God's church?

In 1 Corinthians 1:10–17, Paul explained what long-lasting, God-honoring, world-changing unity is made of.

Ingredient 1: Doctrinal Unity

Doctrinal unity refers to the church believing the same things. While there is certainly room for much discussion and latitude on a number of doctrinal issues, true unity demands that we be in lockstep on many core beliefs of the Christian faith.

You've probably heard it said that "the family that prays together stays together." Well, Paul was saying that the church that believes together sticks together. First Corinthians 1:10 continues, "Now I plead with you, brethren, by the name of our Lord Jesus Christ, that you all speak the same thing, and that there be no *divisions* among you…" (NKJV, emphasis added).

The Greek word for *divisions* is *schisma*. From *schisma*, we get English words like *schism* and *scissors*.[14] Division is the result of something badly torn or deeply cut. This was an injury report on the Corinthians.

Paul reminded them of what a healthy church body can be like: "…that you be perfectly joined together in the same mind and in the same judgment" (1 Corinthians 1:10 NKJV). Those words "perfectly joined together" refer to something that used to be broken but has been fixed, healed, or mended together.[15] It is like a bone that had been broken, but was set and is now healed; a fishing net that had been cut on rocks, but was mended and can be used again; or a garment that had once been torn, but was expertly sewn back together and can now be worn again.

Paul brought encouragement by indicating that healing was possible for the church. You can be made whole. You can be fixed. You can be effective again. It's not too late. And it all begins with doctrinal unity.

Paul explained doctrinal unity in three parts:

- Speaking the same things

- Having the same mind
- Exercising the same judgment.

To speak the same things simply means to agree on the same things. If you are saying the same things, you agree on the same things. If you speak the same things and agree on the same things, what will you have? The same mind.

When we think and speak the same way about things, we will ultimately make the same judgments or decisions. Those decisions and judgments then unite us and help us to move forward together in the same direction.

Similarly, when Paul challenged the church at Philippi to be one, he essentially said, "If you have any joy at all in being a Christian, any mercy at all in your hearts, then think the same way and focus on one goal" (Philippians 2:1–2, paraphrased). A lack of unity reveals that personal kingdoms and agendas have taken precedence and priority over God's kingdom and agenda.

Now, it's important to understand that Paul was not pleading for uniformity in the church. A church with uniformity gathers people from the same socioeconomic class, the same generational background, the same worldview, the same ethnicity, and the same social connections. Uniformity provides a pseudo-unity that cannot bear the weight of the complex challenges brought in when trying to reach people of different ages, backgrounds, beliefs, preferences, and ambitions. Paul was not arguing for uniformity, for everyone in the church to look the same, dress the same, talk the same, sing the same, or act the same. Uniformity deepens immaturity rather than curing it.

Biblical unity is not everyone looking the same, but everyone looking to the same God, who loves all people, created all people, died for all people, and will populate heaven with people from every tongue, tribe, and nation

(Revelation 7:9). In fact, unity is most evident when we are unified with people who are not like us, because then the source of our unity—Jesus—is on full display. Biblical unity means broken people saved by the same God, filled with the same Spirit, proclaiming the same message, pursuing the same mission, and eagerly anticipating an eternity with the One who redeemed them all.

Does this mean that there is no room for discussion or debate among church members about what the Bible says or means? Of course not. Does this mean that we have to agree on every single detail of Christian theology? No. But there are some definite core beliefs regarding which Christians must have the same mind, make the same judgments, and speak the same things.

Strong doctrinal unity is the foundation upon which everything else rests. Without it, we build our churches on the shifting sand of personal experience or cultural values. I agree wholeheartedly with Kevin DeYoung when he tweeted, "Christianity is so much more than getting your doctrine right, but it is not less."[16]

Here are some of the core beliefs many evangelical churches consider critical to a healthy, united church:

- The Bible is the inspired, infallible, inerrant Word of God (2 Timothy 3:16).
- Mankind is sinful and deserves the punishment of God for our sin (Romans 3:23).
- Salvation is through Christ alone, by grace alone, through faith alone (Ephesians 2:8–9).
- God lives within every believer by way of the Holy Spirit (1 Corinthians 6:19).
- Christians are the church and the bride of Christ. God has made us a family that needs one other (Ephesians 2; Revelation 19:7).

- The church is commissioned to live in this sin-filled world as recipients of His grace and advertisements of His great love. We are commanded to tell the world of the good news of Christ (Matthew 28:16–20; 2 Corinthians 5:14–21).
- We are to make disciples and teach them how to obey the Lord through His Word (Matthew 28:19–20).
- Every person has an appointment with death and will then face judgment (Hebrews 9:27).
- Jesus will one day return for His bride, and the church will be with Him forever (Hebrews 9:28).

In one of his classic quotes, R.C. Sproul wrote:[17]

> Theology (or doctrine) is unavoidable for every Christian. It is our attempt to understand the truth that God has revealed to us—something every Christian does. So it is not a question of whether we are going to engage in theology; it is a question of whether our theology is sound or unsound.

Every person is a theologian. The only question is whether we are good theologians or bad theologians. Doctrinal unity in sound theology is necessary for a thriving, vibrant church.

Ingredient 2: Pastoral Unity

True unity starts with harmony in foundational doctrines of the faith, but it continues with pastoral unity, which means that all church members follow and honor the same leader.

> *For it has been declared to me concerning you, my brethren, by those of Chloe's household, that there are contentions among you. Now I say this, that each of you says, "I am of Paul," or "I am of Apollos," or "I am of Cephas," or "I am of Christ." Is Christ divided? Was Paul crucified for you? Or were you baptized in the name of Paul?*
>
> **—1 Corinthians 1:11–13** (NKJV)

The people within the church of Corinth had become unloving, intolerant, and loyal to different leaders. There were at least four factions, four divisions of people. There were individuals who followed Paul only, Apollos only, Cephas only, and Christ only. Clearly, none of those four leaders taught or supported division within the church. The factions were formed by the people who were taking sides and championing their favorite leader while speaking negatively of another. All four groups were equally wrong and sinful.

The Paul Fan Club. First, there was the Paul fan club. These were charter members of the church who remembered the glory days when Paul had come to Corinth and preached, and they were saved. They were there when the church was birthed, so they had a special affinity for Paul, their spiritual father. Their faith was grown in the crucible of adversity. They loved Paul and saw him as their perfect leader.

Their fervent love for Paul allowed them to overlook some of his weaknesses. In 1 Corinthians 2:1, Paul wrote, "And so it was with me, brothers and sisters. When I came to you, I did not come with eloquence or human wisdom as I proclaimed to you the testimony about God." Paul was neither a polished speaker nor overly captivating. Not everyone in the church of Corinth was enamored with Pastor Paul.

The Apollos Fan Club. The Apollos fan club consisted of the second-generation Christians saved under the ministry of the second pastor of Corinth, Apollos. He followed Paul but was very different from him. Apollos was a tremendous orator, who captivated people with his powerful preaching and intellect:

> *Meanwhile, a Jew named Apollos, an eloquent speaker who knew the Scriptures well, had arrived in Ephesus from Alexandria in Egypt. He had been taught the way of the Lord, and* ***he taught others about Jesus with an enthusiastic spirit and with accuracy****. ... He refuted the Jews with powerful arguments in public debate. Using the Scriptures, he explained to them that Jesus was the Messiah.*
>
> ***—Acts 18:24–25, 28*** ***(NLT, emphasis added)***

Paul was gifted by God in one way; Apollos was gifted by God in another way. But rather than appreciating the gifts of these men and glorifying God, the church members split into fan clubs and focused on supporting their respective favorite.

The Cephas (Simon Peter) Fan Club. The apostle Peter was probably the most well-known disciple of Jesus and had preached as an itinerant preacher. It was considered a huge win if you joined under him.

The Jesus Fan Club. This team sounds like the best team to be part of, doesn't it? However, that wasn't the case. These people thought of themselves as "super saints" who needed no one but Jesus, and they refused to be held accountable by any pastoral authority. They wanted to do things as they pleased, when they pleased, and how they pleased. They wanted the privileges of the church without the responsibilities. They wanted to enjoy the wonder of Sunday morning without doing the work of the rest of the week. They wanted the blessing of ministry but weren't willing to carry the burden. "You can count on us when it's time to eat, but not when it's time to cook. We'll be there for the singing, but not for the serving."

The church today is full of similar people who want the blessing of obedience without actually obeying. They are unwilling to commit, to work, to submit, to serve, to give, to endure, and to sacrifice. "Don't tell me what to do. Don't tell me when to come. Don't tell me how to live. Don't tell me to deny myself. If you do, I'll go somewhere where they will press less, preach less, and expect less." This attitude runs rampant in the church.

At first glance, this last group appears the most spiritual, but it is actually the most repugnant and the most arrogant. Sadly, the American church is filled with the very worst of what the Corinthian church had just a fraction of: perpetual visitors hopscotching the city, hoping that the latest and greatest church fad will fill their void. The result is a severe lack in depth of relationship and commitment to vision.

Hebrews 13:17 is a sharp rebuke to this pervasive attitude that rejects pastoral leadership:

> *Have confidence in your leaders and submit to their authority, because they keep watch over you as those who must give an account. Do this so that their work will be a joy, not a burden, for that would be of no benefit to you.*

The Bible clearly calls Christians to submit and commit to the spiritual leaders given to them by God.

> *And He Himself gave some to be apostles, some prophets, some evangelists, and some pastors and teachers, for the equipping of the saints for the work of ministry, for the edifying of the body of Christ, till we all come to the unity of*

the faith and of the knowledge of the Son of God....
***—Ephesians 4:11–13** (NKJV)*

God calls some to be pastors leading His church. He equips them with His power to preach His Word and lead His way. He says to the church, "They are Mine. Follow them. As you follow them and they follow Me, you, too, are following Me."

In critiquing the Corinthians' fan-club approach to following, Paul wasn't preaching against human leaders and pastors in the church. Later, in 1 Corinthians 11:1, he wrote, "Imitate me, just as I also imitate Christ" (NKJV). Paul was saying, "Remember that Jesus died for you. He saved you. You were buried in Christ, not in me, so don't divide up your heart and loyalty. Give your heart and loyalty to Christ, but then be unified in following your God-chosen, God-given, God-gifted pastor, whom He has clearly put right in front of you. Be unified in what you believe and in whom you follow."

Pastors will be held accountable for how wisely they lead. Likewise, every Christian will be held accountable for how humbly he or she follows. It takes deep commitment to both leadership and followership for a church to stick together through the storms it will inevitably face.

Ingredient 3: Missional Unity

A unified church is full of Christ-followers living for the same mission and pursuing the same purpose. Paul wrote:

I thank God that I baptized none of you except Crispus and Gaius, lest anyone should say that I had baptized in my own name. Yes, I also baptized the household of Stephanas. Besides, I do not know whether I baptized any other. For

> *Christ did not send me to baptize,* ***but to preach the gospel,*** *not with wisdom of words, lest the cross of Christ should be made of no effect.*
>
> ***—1 Corinthians 1:14–17*** ***(NKJV, emphasis added)***

Paul was not against baptism. He experienced it, preached it, and practiced it. The problem wasn't baptism, but the pride people displayed because of *who* baptized them. Paul was saying, "Baptism is fine, but that's not why I'm here, and that's not why you're here. We're here to preach the gospel." The unity God wanted required them to possess the same priority and pursue the same purpose.

Jesus gave us our missional mandate:

> *Go therefore and make* ***disciples*** *of all the nations, baptizing them in the name of the Father and of the Son and of the Holy Spirit, teaching them to observe all things that I have commanded you; and lo, I am with you always, even to the end of the age.*
>
> ***—Matthew 28:19–20*** ***(NKJV, emphasis added)***

The imperative here is obvious. Everywhere we go and in every way we can, we are to make disciples of Jesus Christ through His good news. The mission of every church is to fulfill the Great Commission of Jesus.

What Is at Stake

Why is unity such an important characteristic in the church? Because unity is an important characteristic of the Trinity. God the Father, God the Son, and God the Holy Spirit are in perfect unity with one another. Though they're three distinct Persons, they are one God. They hold different roles individually, but they have the same goals corporately.

The church in the world is to reflect the nature of the Trinity. When the rest of the world can't seem to agree on anything or stand to be around people who are different from them, a church in which natural enemies become brothers and sisters in Christ is a powerful witness. Unity is a visible manifestation of a Spirit-empowered church. Christians, like the Triune God, must embrace their unique characteristics and, at the same time, pursue the same goals of the Kingdom.

When Unity Is Lacking

If our unity reflects the Trinity, our disunity brings dishonor to God's character. When we have disunity, we distort a proper understanding of God. When we have division, we lose credibility with unbelievers. Unity is absolutely necessary for us to complete the mission for which we are still here.

Jesus made it clear to His church just how important true unity and togetherness in the church are in His last prayer before going to the cross:

> *I will remain in the world no longer, but they are still in the world, and I am coming to you. Holy Father, protect them by the power of your name, the name you gave me, so that they may be one as we are one. ... My prayer is not for them alone. I pray also for those who will believe in me through their message, that all of them may be one, Father, just as you are in me and I am in you. May they also be in us so that the world may believe that you have sent me. I have given them the glory that you gave me, that they may be one as we are one—I in them and you in me—so that they may be brought to complete unity.* ***Then the world will know that you sent me and have loved them even as you have loved me.***
>
> *—John 17:11, 20–23* (emphasis added)

Unity makes God's gospel more attractive to a searching person and more believable to a watching world. A void of togetherness in a church does the opposite. A bickering, divided church is a spiritually weak and missionally ineffective church.

You see, a lack of doctrinal unity, a lack of strongly believing the same way regarding the core essentials of the Christian faith, can cause us to go in different directions. When we begin to think differently, decide differently, and speak differently, unity in the church cannot exist. When you can't agree on the important things, there's no way you'll agree on unimportant things. Churches implode over music, worship style, building colors, pastor salaries, decision-making rights, and other significant but morally neutral issues because they are not united on the most important matters that cannot be negotiated.

Unity begins by recognizing that all believers are *already* one because we were all made right with God the same way and bought by God with the same blood, the blood of Jesus. Galatians 3:28 reminds us, "There is neither Jew nor Gentile, neither slave nor free, nor is there male and female, for you are *all one* in Christ Jesus" (emphasis added). We're not called to create unity; we are called to preserve it. We don't have to provide unity; we are to protect it. We do so by loving one another, serving one another, forgiving one another, blessing one another, learning with one another, and being humble toward one another.

When we have the same fundamental beliefs and the same missional priorities, accurately derived from God's Word, our unity overrides our preferences, personalities, temperaments, and opinions. Then we are able to focus on Christ and others rather than on ourselves.

It's tempting to ignore divisiveness instead of addressing its destructiveness. Many treatable diseases can spread throughout our physical bodies if they are ignored and left untreated. If a growth of abnormal cells is ignored, it can become a cancerous tumor that may potentially kill the afflicted person. Likewise, if church conflict is ignored, it can affect people both spiritually and relationally.

It only takes one fly in the ointment to ruin the whole batch. It only takes one church member to get out of sorts, get loose with his or her lips, and let the flesh take control to allow the cancer of conflict to start growing in the body. We cannot afford to allow a handful of people who are willing to sacrifice unity for the sake of petty issues to go unchallenged.

When Unity Is Present

Do you know what Jesus said would be evidence that a person loves God, serves God, and belongs to God? Jesus said, "Blessed are the peacemakers, for they will be called children of God" (Matthew 5:9). We only become children of God through the substitutionary work of Jesus Christ on the cross and His resurrection from the dead. Jesus made the only way for us to experience forgiveness and peace with God. We demonstrate that we belong to Him and that He lives in us when we have a passion for living in peace with others. As the writer of Hebrews plainly stated, "Make every effort to *live in peace* with everyone and to be holy; without holiness no one will see the Lord" (Hebrews 12:14, emphasis added).

Isn't it interesting that Jesus washed the feet of all twelve of His closest disciples, even though only eleven were truly for Him (John 13)? It's impossible to look down on a person when you are washing his feet. Judas had his dirty, wandering feet washed by the perfectly pure Son of God. He even sat next to Jesus at the supper table, a recognized place of special honor. At one point, Jesus dipped a piece of bread and served it to Judas, a sign of deep love and intimacy (John 13:18). Jesus performed all of these gracious acts of love for a man He knew would betray Him and hand Him over to a group of bloodthirsty religious leaders for a handful of silver coins.

I doubt that many of us will be asked to go that far for another church member. However, whenever we decide that a brother or sister in Christ is too wrong or too sinful for us to serve humbly or understand patiently, we need to remember how Jesus treated Judas. Does anyone come to mind for you right now? Let's not forget what Jesus taught and modeled for us. We are to love even our enemies.

Will You Fight or Unite?

A visitor went to an asylum for the criminally insane and was surprised to find that there were only three guards to take care of a hundred inmates. He said to one of the guards, "Aren't you afraid that the inmates will band together, overcome you, and escape?" The guard dryly replied, "There is no such fear. Lunatics never unite."[18]

The church has a choice. We can either fight among ourselves or band together and unite. Which will you choose?

WORKBOOK

Chapter One Questions

Question: What do you see as the greatest problems in the American church today? Do you, like Paul, rank division and dissension near the top? Why or why not? Does most of the division and dissension you see relate to non-negotiable doctrinal issues or to preferences and personal rights?

____

____

____

____

____

____

____

____

____

____

____

____

Question: Does your congregation know, understand, and embrace your church's essential beliefs and mission statement? How can you regularly and creatively instruct the church in these key doctrinal points to make sure that every person, young and old, knows and can defend these core beliefs?

____

____

____

____

____

____

____

____

____

____

____

____

Question: Where and why do you see the "Lone Ranger Christian" mentality popping up in churches today? How does this affect church unity? What are some practical ways that pastors and Christian leaders can combat this attitude and foster a commitment to accountability, unity, and community?

____

____

____

____

____

____

____

____

____

____

____

____

Action: Make or look up a list of the "one anothers" in Scripture (e.g., "love one another," "forgive one another," "serve one another"). How can you regularly incorporate these succinct and powerful reminders into your own life and that of your small group or church?

Chapter One Notes

CHAPTER TWO

The Sides: Team Meat and Team No Meat

Now about food sacrificed to idols: We know that "We all possess knowledge." But knowledge puffs up while love builds up. Those who think they know something do not yet know as they ought to know. But whoever loves God is known by God.

—1 Corinthians 8:1–3

Who am I? Beloved by God. He loves me more than I love Him, and now I get to love other people more than they love me.[19]

—Ed T. Welch

Some things just aren't what they appear to be. I read that there are nearly eight million cats in New York City. Part of the challenge of being a cat owner in the Big Apple is figuring out what to do with the cat's remains after it dies. Most people don't have a backyard, and it's illegal to bury cats in the local parks. What is a cat owner to do? Well, the city provides a service: for fifty dollars, they will come retrieve and deal with your dearly departed cat.

One entrepreneurial woman came up with the clever idea to take care of the problem for half the price. She placed an ad in the newspaper that read: "When your cat dies, I'll remove it for twenty-five dollars."

The calls came rolling in. Each time, the woman went to a local Goodwill or Salvation Army store to purchase an old suitcase for two or three dollars. She then went to the client's residence and carefully placed the dead cat in the suitcase.

In the early evening, during the peak time for thieves and pickpockets, she took a ride on the subway. She sat near a set of doors, put the suitcase down next to her, and pretended she wasn't paying attention. Inevitably, a thief would approach her. When the train stopped and the doors opened, the thief would quickly grab the suitcase and run away.

The woman, rather unenthusiastically, shouted, "Stop, thief! Stop!" I wish we had video footage of the thieves' reactions upon opening those suitcases. No doubt those thieves would agree that some things just aren't what they appear to be.[20]

Idols, Meat, and Market—Oh My!

Most Christians in the United States will never have to face the issue of whether to eat meat that has been offered to an idol. Therefore, it might seem that spending time thinking about this matter is foolish, but it would be a mistake to ignore the importance of this conflict in the Corinthian church. Believe me, like that suitcase on the subway, there is more here than "meats" the eye.

The Problem: To Eat or Not to Eat

Despite its overt depravity, Corinth was a remarkably

religious city. The temples of all the pagan gods were filled with people and priests offering animal sacrifice as a means of worship.

This is how it worked. A person took a chicken or a cow to the temple, and the priest cut the meat into three parts for three purposes:

1. One part was burned on the altar to the pagan gods.
2. One part was sold by the priest in the market for money.
3. One part was given back to the family to take home and eat.

Consequently, any time you bought meat at the market or ate at a friend's house, it was highly probable that the meat had been sacrificed in worship to a false god.

The pagan temples themselves also presented a confounding dilemma for the Corinthian Christians. They not only were places of worship, but served as social venues as well. If you were going to have a birthday party, a sports banquet, a retirement bash, or a wedding celebration, you could rent out the hall at a local temple and hold your festivities there.[21] As you can see, going to the temples of these pagan gods was a normal part of life, woven into the very fabric of Corinthian society.

Imagine living in first-century Corinth, a city saturated with idolatry. The temples have become a hub for community life. They are where you buy meat for supper. They are where you go to pray. You would even have been married at one of the temples.

Then, one day, you hear a man named Paul preaching that there is only one God, who sent His Son, Jesus, from heaven to earth. You hear how Jesus came from heaven, lived a perfect life to fulfill God's law, died a sacrificial death for the sins of mankind, rose from the dead to provide eternal life, and now rescues people from eternal doom and death when they repent of their sin and put their faith in Him. Almost instantly, God grabs your heart and illuminates your mind, and you believe, repent, surrender, and are saved. You've never experienced such internal peace and joy.

Now, quite suddenly, because of your commitment to Christ, you are expected to turn your back on all of the idolatry, worship, and activities associated with the temples dedicated to false gods. This undoubtedly posed a profound challenge for the Corinthian Christians.

This was no small thing. It wasn't just a matter of changing worship locations. The decision to follow Christ meant a radical change to the new Christians' family lives, worship lives, business lives, and social lives. Every aspect of their lives was connected to those temples and their gods.

This was a serious struggle for the Corinthian Christians because it forced them to avoid events and festivities in which they had previously participated. They had to do things that seemed strange to their friends and family. "No, I can't go to the work party at the temple of Aphrodite." "No, we won't be coming to the garden grounds of Asclepios' shrine for the family reunion." "No, we won't be getting married in the House of Hermes." "We won't condone anything having to do with those false gods." Consequently, the Christians would have been seen as weird, inconsiderate, or even antisocial.

The Solutions: Team Meat Versus Team No Meat

But the bigger dilemma came from inside the church. The chasm between the Christians who ate the sacrificed meat and those who didn't continued to deepen.

The meat eaters (Team Meat) were considered more

spiritually mature by the apostle Paul. As their faith and spiritual insight grew, they began to realize that maybe it wouldn't be so wrong to go to the temples or to buy the meat offered to Aphrodite or the other temple gods.

Their expanding spiritual knowledge enabled them to understand that there is only one true God; thus, the idols around them were not real. They didn't exist. Nonexistent gods could not possibly contaminate the meat sacrificed to them (1 Corinthians 8:4–6). If the gods weren't real and the meat wasn't tainted, what was the harm in eating it? None, they reasoned.

On the opposing side, the non-meat eaters (Team No Meat) were considered by Paul to be the less mature believers. They were appalled at the idea of eating meat sacrificed to idols and vehemently opposed it. To them, eating that meat was a horrible sin. They used to visit those temples, offer that meat, and worship those idols. But God graciously and miraculously saved them out of that lifestyle, and they wanted absolutely nothing to do with it. They earnestly warned the meat eaters to sever ties with the meat as well, but the meat eaters did not want to listen.

These opposing convictions caused major friction in the Corinthian church, and as a result, the Corinthians sought the wise counsel of the apostle Paul. "Can we eat this meat in the temples of the false gods as long as we don't worship them?" they asked.

While the Corinthians wanted a yes *or* no answer, Paul gave them a yes *and* no answer. Their question for Paul was so poignant and significant that it took him three chapters to answer it (1 Corinthians 8–10).

When Knowledge Puffs Up

Now about food sacrificed to idols: We know that "We all

possess knowledge."

—1 Corinthians 8:1

Paul repeated the Corinthians' words to address the issue of food sacrificed to idols. In their letter, they asserted that Paul didn't have the market cornered on spiritual knowledge. "We all possess knowledge," they argued. There was a bite to their comment.

Paul responded by saying, "Yes, yes. I know that we all have knowledge." Then, he lowered the boom in the second half of verse 1: "But knowledge puffs up while love builds up." Paul used the phrase "puffs up" to mean "to inflate with pride." Before he dealt with the Corinthians' public behavior, he shone a light on their inward attitude. He told them that they were theologically correct but relationally wrong.

> Knowledge is proud that it knows so much; wisdom is humble that it knows no more.[22]
>
> **—William Cowper**

Instead of this wonderful new knowledge from God deepening their humility about who they were in Christ, they allowed it to inflate their pride about who they were in the church. Their spiritual knowledge led them to feel superior to other Christians. Consequently, their knowledge was stifling the church rather than strengthening it.

It's important to realize that there is nothing wrong with having an abundance of spiritual knowledge. Christianity is not an anti-intellectual movement. God never blesses ignorance. In fact, God encourages us to pursue and possess knowledge because a lack of knowledge is spiritually devastating:

- "Therefore my people have gone into captivity, because they have no knowledge" (Isaiah 5:13 NKJV).
- "My people are destroyed for lack of knowledge. Because you have rejected knowledge, I also will reject you from being priest for Me; because you have forgotten the law of your God, I also will forget your children" (Hosea 4:6 NKJV). What you don't know can hurt you, and it can hurt those you lead and love.
- "Wise people store up knowledge" (Proverbs 10:14 NKJV).
- "Get wisdom! Get understanding! Do not forget, nor turn away from the words of my mouth" (Proverbs 4:5 NKJV).

Paul's point to the Corinthians could not have been to stop gaining knowledge or deepening their insight. These qualities are crucial to the Christian life. Jesus said, "Then you will know the truth, and the truth will set you free" (John 8:32).

When Knowledge Lacks Love

The underlying problem for the first-century Corinthians is the same for many twenty-first-century Christians: too much knowledge with too little application. They had acquired the knowledge, but they refused to employ it. Their spiritual knowledge extended beyond their level of personal obedience.

Not one of us has *too much* knowledge of the Bible; trouble comes when it has *too little* effect on our daily lives. Paul's admonishment to the people of Corinth, and to all Christians, was that knowledge is *essential* but not *sufficient*. He wrote, "Those who think they know something do not yet know as they ought to know" (1 Corinthians 8:2). The process cannot stop with our brains; it must move through our hearts and on to our hands and feet.

While knowledge is necessary, knowledge that sticks to the mind but doesn't touch the heart is dangerous and detrimental. Knowledge can inflate an individual ego, but love is what builds up an entire church.

Knowledge without love makes you arrogant and argumentative. Some Christians would rather be right about a spiritual subject than right with their spiritual family. They'd rather win an argument than keep a friend. They prefer knowing more than others to getting along with others. They have allowed their heavenly knowledge to blind them to their demonic pride.

Paul later wrote, "And though I have the gift of prophecy, and understand all mysteries and all knowledge, and though I have all faith, so that I could remove mountains, but have not love, I am nothing" (1 Corinthians 13:2 NKJV).

That's the picture of a Christian who knows much but loves little. Christians who damage the church often have a full head but an empty heart. They love to argue about deep theological principles in their small group, but they show little interest in caring humbly for their small-group members when needs arise. The popular saying is correct: "People don't care how much you know until they know how much you care." Knowledge without love inflates your ego and hurts others, but knowledge with love helps you to grow and benefits others.

In 1 Corinthians 8:3, Paul made this piercing point: "But whoever loves God is known by God." Notice Paul didn't say that if you know many Bible verses, you are known by God. No, because it's not about a transfer of information; it's about a demonstration of love. The Bible informs you about God to ignite a love for God. If you love God, you are known by Him. When your love for God is attached to your knowledge of God, it creates something awesome. It creates a relationship. Your love for God shows that you truly know God. More importantly, it reveals that He knows you.

Let me illustrate. It would be one thing for me to tell you that I know the actor Denzel Washington (I wish!). You may or may not be impressed. But it would be quite different if Denzel knew me, and you heard him mention me by name in an interview on TV. It's not merely that I know him. If he also knows me, it makes all the difference in the world. That makes it a genuine, two-way relationship.

The God Who Knows Us

Paul said that when you know God with your mind and love Him with your heart, you know that He knows you. That's the knowledge faith is made of. The all-powerful Creator and Sustainer of everything knows you intimately and thoroughly.

Because of the atoning work of Jesus through the cross, God sees you as His very own beloved child. Despite all of the junk we have, all of the messes we've made, and all of the harm we've done, He sent His Son to cover it all and wash us clean forever.

That spiritual knowledge should make us humble, not prideful. It should make us love others more, not less. The spiritual knowledge in our minds must be counterbalanced with the love of God in our hearts, or else pride will find its way in.

Those who truly love God have a heart that desperately wants to obey Him and serve others. They are not consumed with their position in the church but with God's purpose for the church. Ed Welch said it beautifully:[23]

> Love refuses to be a mere observer but insists on being a friend who is brought into the story and, with compassion, is affected by it.

Truly loving people will not want to hoard their knowledge of God's Word for themselves; they will find a way to share it. Someone who is truly loving will use his or her surplus resources to meet the needs of others. For example, a loving person who has the ability and opportunity to encourage a hurting friend will certainly pay that friend a visit. Knowledge that isn't funneled into sacrificial service is useless and stands as a witness to our pitiful pride.

Need a daily example of extreme brilliance combined with godly love leading to humble service? "This is how we know what love is: Jesus Christ laid down his life for us. And we ought to lay down our lives for our brothers and sisters" (1 John 3:16). Jesus lovingly laid down His life for our salvation. Now we lovingly lay down our lives because of it.

The Corinthians thought that they had a meat problem when they actually had a love problem. Meat didn't cause disunity; it revealed it. Whatever problem is pulling your heart away from other believers or dividing your local church comes from the same root issue. There are no problems too big to solve, just people who have not grown enough in love to solve them.

WORKBOOK

Chapter Two Questions

Question: What are some ways that Christians today stand out (or should stand out) against the cultural norms? Have you ever been considered weird or inconsiderate, even antisocial, because of your standards as a Christian? What are some ways that living a countercultural life varies by nation and location?

____

____

____

____

____

____

____

____

____

____

Question: Name three specific divisions or contentions within your own church and/or denomination that have no clear biblical guideline but must be sorted out based on the biblical principles that Paul taught the Corinthians. Would you be excited, nervous, or defensive about discussing these matters with leaders of your church? Why?

____

____

____

____

____

____

____

____

____

____

____

____

Question: Describe a time in your ministry or the ministry of someone you have observed when knowledge crushed the church rather than strengthening it. What attitudes behind this knowledge caused it to be destructive rather than instructive?

____

____

____

____

____

____

____

____

____

____

____

____

Action: On a separate piece of paper, draw two columns and contrast *knowledge with love* and *knowledge without love*. Which column best characterizes your current attitude, leadership style, church culture, and immediate family?

Chapter Two Notes

CHAPTER THREE

The First Quandary: Am I My Brother's Keeper?

But food does not bring us near to God; we are no worse if we do not eat, and no better if we do.

Be careful, however, that the exercise of your rights does not become a stumbling block to the weak. For if someone with a weak conscience sees you, with all your knowledge, eating in an idol's temple, won't that person be emboldened to eat what is sacrificed to idols? So this weak brother or sister, for whom Christ died, is destroyed by your knowledge.

—1 Corinthians 8:8–11

The man who attempts Christianity without the church shoots himself in the foot, shoots his children in the leg, and shoots his grandchildren in the heart.[24]

—Kevin DeYoung

In July 2005, the Pittsburgh Steelers' rookie quarterback Ben Roethlisberger was asked by ESPN reporter Andrea Kremer to defend his decision to ride his motorcycle without wearing a helmet. Roethlisberger answered, "I don't wear a helmet because I don't have to. It's not the law. If it was the law, I'd definitely have one on every time I rode. But it's not the law and I know I don't have to. You're just freer when you're out there with no helmet on."

Unfortunately, Roethlisberger was involved in a serious motorcycle accident almost a year later in June of 2006.[25] A sixty-two-year-old woman failed to yield at an intersection, and Roethlisberger was thrown into the windshield of her car. His bike was smashed, and surgeons spent over seven hours repairing a broken jaw, a fractured skull, missing teeth, and several other facial injuries.[26]

After his hospital release, Roethlisberger humbly apologized to the fans, his family, and his team for taking unnecessary risks with his health and his life. In a later interview, he was no longer determined to take advantage of his individual freedom: "In the past few days, I've gained a new perspective on life. By the grace of God, I'm fortunate to be alive." He also added that if he ever decided to ride a motorcycle again, "It will certainly be with a helmet."[27]

Roethlisberger, a self-proclaimed Christian, had the freedom to ride his motorcycle without a helmet, but doing so endangered his life and potentially the lives of many others. How is that? Well, one might argue that if Ben Roethlisberger, the youngest quarterback ever to win a Super Bowl, doesn't need to wear a helmet, why should I? Tens of thousands of people watched this interview on ESPN, and some might have pursued his kind of "freedom."[28]

We Are Our Brothers' Keepers

Spiritually speaking, the apostle Paul warned us not to

make the same type of mistake and lead fellow believers into attitudes and actions that could severely damage their walk with God and the health of the local church. Let's not kid ourselves: we are our brothers' keepers. Practically, this implies that there are certain behaviors and activities we should choose not to participate in, even if they are permissible for us, out of love for our fellow believers and the mission of Jesus' church.

Let me explain. There are certain actions that the Bible says are wrong for everyone, such as murder, lying, cheating, stealing, and idolatry. There are certain actions that are right for everyone, such as honesty, fidelity, and sexual purity. These issues could be called black-and-white areas. However, there are many issues and actions on which the Bible does not take an absolute stance. You could describe these as gray areas.

Gray areas are issues on which Scripture does not take a dogmatic stance or issues that Scripture does not discuss in depth. We might consider these actions and practices neutral. Grasping what these specific areas are in our own lives and obediently following the guidance of the Spirit for the advancement of His gospel are at the heart of this book.

My "Rights" and Your Good

In Chapter One, we addressed Paul's first principle of realizing the destructive nature of knowledge without love. Paul's second principle focuses on the possibility that an individual's rights can cause spiritual harm to others. Paul began this line of thought with 1 Corinthians 8:4: "So then, about eating food sacrificed to idols: We know that 'An idol is nothing at all in the world' and that 'There is no God but one.'" Paul, as earlier in the passage, quoted the Corinthians and agreed with their knowledge.

Then he pressed a little further:

> *For even if there are so-called gods, whether in heaven or on earth (as indeed there are many "gods" and many "lords"), yet for us there is but one God, the Father, from whom all things came and for whom we live; and there is but one Lord, Jesus Christ, through whom all things came and through whom we live.*
>
> ***—1 Corinthians 8:5–6***

Once again, Paul agreed with their theological conviction by confirming, "Yes, there is only one God the Father, and there is only one Lord, Jesus Christ." Then he was ready to expose the hidden problem lurking in those convictions:

> *But not everyone possesses this knowledge. Some people are still so accustomed to idols that when they eat sacrificial food they think of it as having been sacrificed to a god, and since their conscience is weak, it is defiled. But food does not bring us near to God; we are no worse if we do not eat, and no better if we do.*
>
> ***—1 Corinthians 8:7–8***

"But not everyone possesses this knowledge."

Paul confirmed the belief of the meat eaters that food cannot be contaminated by something that is not legitimate (1 Corinthians 8:4, 8). Whether or not a big building is dedicated to a nonexistent god is meaningless. The meat eaters were absolutely right about this knowledge, but they were squarely wrong when they said that *all* Christians possess this knowledge. You see, though idols aren't real, idolatry is.

A weaker believer can be lured into sin by a mere idea that may or may not be true. Thoughts don't have to be true to be powerful. This is a favorite battleground of our enemy, the devil. Addressing the more mature Corinthian

Christians, Paul agreed that they may have been able to go to a temple without even thinking about the false god and eat meat sacrificed to an idol with a clear conscience, because they knew that this so-called god didn't exist and that eating the meat did not have any negative consequences.

However, the weaker or less-mature Christians were unable to act in the same manner. When they went into that temple or ate that meat, the spiritual result was reverting to thoughts and ways that reflected their old lives of idolatry, not their new lives in Christ.

The less-mature believers allowed an old behavior framed in a new perspective to lead them away from Christ. They had yet to grasp the divine knowledge that idols were nothing. Consequently, that idol was very real for them. Adults know that the bogeyman isn't real, but the terror that the thought of him creates in the heart of a child is very real.

For some of the Corinthians, idols that weren't real led them into idolatrous thoughts and feelings that were very real. In eating meat that had been sacrificed to idols, the weaker believers, believing in their hearts that they were sinning against God, defiled their consciences.

The more mature Corinthian Christians had grown into the proper understanding that the gospel gave them immense freedom. This knowledge about false gods gave them the liberty to go to various temples and eat meat sacrificed to idols without stepping into sin or misrepresenting their faith. They reasoned, "It doesn't damage our walk with Christ, nor lead us into any sinful habits. This God-given knowledge gives us the green light to go to the temple and eat that meat without any fear or guilt." They figured that if it was right for them, it must be right for all. It was at this juncture that they were wrong.

Don't let your rights become a "stumbling block."

The problem occurred when Team Meat did not make love the highest priority, and as a result, they quickly went from "my knowledge" to "my rights." Their rights were negatively affecting other believers who didn't possess the same knowledge or maturity. Paul was saying to them, "Your rights have become a stumbling block to other believers." He wrote:

> *Be careful, however, that the exercise of your rights does not become a stumbling block to the weak. For if someone with a weak conscience sees you, with all your knowledge, eating in an idol's temple, won't that person be emboldened to eat what is sacrificed to idols? So this weak brother or sister, for whom Christ died,* ***is destroyed*** *by your knowledge.*
>
> ***—1 Corinthians 8:9–11*** *(emphasis added)*

Paul didn't say that your rights disappoint or distract other believers. He emphatically said that this knowledge destroys the less-mature believers. This is not eternal spiritual destruction, but rather a serious setback in spiritual growth. The weaker believers didn't lose their salvation from God; they lost their fellowship with Him. It led them away from Christ and back toward idolatry, which always brings spiritual calamity and dysfunction. Paul admonished Team Meat that their knowledge may have given them the right to eat the meat sacrificed to idols, but it didn't give them the right to tear down fellow believers' consciences and lead them astray.

Our actions influence others, whether we realize it or not. What may not negatively affect your faith could destroy someone else's. God says that is a right you don't have permission to exercise. Weaker believers sincerely trying to grow deserve every sacrifice we can make for them. Let me repeat this biblical truth: *we are our brothers' keepers*.

Now, you may be hard-pressed to figure out how this issue affects you. You might be saying, "Bob, I understand what you're saying, but I don't know how this applies to me. I don't live in a part of the world where eating meat that's been sacrificed to idols is an issue. This isn't a problem for me or anyone I know." Let me show you how relevant this passage truly is for all of us.

The Bible gives Christians the liberty to make God-glorifying decisions based on our convictions. These convictions become a matter of personal spiritual preference. While these preferences are not necessarily wrong or sinful for one Christian, they could be wrong or sinful for another. Therefore, we take these convictions and preferences and create what I call a personal "rights box."

The Rights Box

Each of us has a personal, internal, spiritual rights box. In my rights box are the things I believe to be permissible, allowable, and perfectly justified for me within my Christian liberties and walk with God. I can do these things with a pure heart and clean conscience, without sinning against my Savior in the least. Now, the contents of every Christian's rights box are different, and that's where many Christians struggle.

This is a major reason why there are so many different church denominations today. People with similar contents in their rights boxes tend to congregate together. If pressed, most of us could make a list of personal rights and liberties we have placed in our Christian rights box that others haven't.

These rights might include things like listening to secular music, watching R-rated movies, kissing before marriage, playing violent video games, supporting a specific political party, drinking alcohol, telling your children that Santa Claus is real, taking your kids trick-or-treating, working on Sundays, or both parents working outside of the home. The list could go on forever.

Some of you see nothing wrong with anything on that list. Others of you doubt the salvation of anyone who would do such things. Believe it or not, nothing included on that short list is expressly forbidden in Scripture. Each of these items is an issue of personal conviction and conscience based on how God is directing each individual for his or her own good and His eternal glory.

We must remember that each of us answers to God, and He expects us to obey what He tells us. To help give greater clarity to this issue, let me share some examples from my own life.

Example: Drinking

As a pastor, I have seen firsthand the horrific damage alcohol has done to many individuals and families. Personally, I don't think that it's a sin to consume alcohol in moderation, but that is not a liberty you'll find in my rights box. I don't feel the freedom from God to drink alcohol. My conviction is that if I drink alcohol in public, I will likely cause other brothers and sisters to stumble in their personal walks with God and possibly suffer the catastrophic consequences of alcohol abuse.

The argument could be made that if I, a trusted pastor, have an alcoholic beverage every once in a while, that must mean it's acceptable for everyone else to do the same. However, I know that if I were to sit in a restaurant with a glass of wine, I would be defiling my conscience and sinning against God. How? James, the half-brother of Jesus, explained it well: "So whoever knows the right thing to do and fails to do it, *for him* it is sin" (James 4:17 ESV, emphasis added).

Don't miss that: "for him it is sin." It all goes back to our conscience and convictions, steered by the Holy Spirit. The conscience is the part of the human psyche that stimulates mental anguish and causes feelings of guilt when we go against it. Likewise, it invokes feelings of satisfaction and well-being when our actions conform to our internal value system.

Your conscience is a gift from God that allows you to exercise self-evaluation. However, it is a servant of your internal value system. A weak value system with little or no understanding of God's Word or ways will produce a weak conscience. A strong value system fueled by God's Word and Spirit produces a strong conscience. A constantly maturing faith is, therefore, critical for every believer. A maturing faith produces a stronger, godlier conscience.

The apostle Paul made this same point to the Roman Christians when he wrote, "Each one should be fully convinced in his own mind. … But whoever has doubts is condemned if he eats, because the eating is not from faith. For whatever does not proceed from faith is sin" (Romans 14:5, 23 ESV).

Concerning the consumption of alcohol, God has clearly and personally instructed my conscience in this matter. I am fully convinced that it is forbidden for me to drink alcohol. Now, it may be that you know drunkenness is wrong, so you steer clear of that line, but you have no problem at all having a glass of wine publicly or privately. It does not violate your conscience in the least. It's a right you exercise. It's a freedom you enjoy. What is a sin for me is not necessarily a sin for you.

Example: Purchasing a New Vehicle

Personally, I have no problem with having a new car. If someone were to give me a new car, I'd drive it. It wouldn't be sinful; it would be delightful! I've bought several new cars over the years. Some people, however, may believe that buying a new car is a waste of God's money or consider it bad stewardship. Some might even consider it sinful. They would be violating their conscience, as God has convicted them to use their money to build His kingdom, not to acquire an expensive new car. So, rather than purchasing new cars, they buy used cars to give as much to the work of Christ as possible.

Now, let's say that you're a newer, less-mature believer than I am, and I have the privilege of personally discipling you and being an influence on your spiritual growth. What if you had a personal conviction about driving a new car and felt that it was not in your rights box to purchase one, but I came to you and said, "Hey, a new car isn't sinful. You work hard. You can afford it. You already give to the church and the work of God. Loosen up, dude. God is good! Buy a new car. Enjoy!"

Guess what I have done with those few words. I've imposed my freedoms on you. I've allowed my rights to get you to sin against your convictions and your conscience. I've selfishly allowed my rights to become a stumbling block to you.

Example: Secular Music

I enjoy listening to some secular music. Don't tell anyone, but sometimes I even like it loud! But some people are convinced that any song that doesn't have the name of Jesus in it is sinful and satanic. They choose not to listen to anything that isn't considered "Christian music."

If I know people who have trouble with secular music because it takes them back to their wild days of sex, drugs, and rock and roll, and I know that God has convicted them to refrain from listening to it for their spiritual health, I'm not going to turn up my car stereo and blast secular music when they're with me. I'm not going to go to a rock concert and then plaster pictures of it all over their Facebook feeds. I'm also not going to try to convince them to loosen up and rock out every once in a while.

I refuse to let my rights become a stumbling block to other believers. I'm going to tell them to stick to their guns and obey God in their lives. And when I'm with them, I will refrain from exercising that freedom in my rights box. Why? Because I love them more than I love secular music. I will not flaunt my freedom at the expense of their faith.

Love Trumps Your Rights

The Bible is abundantly clear: love trumps my rights, and love limits my liberties. First Corinthians 10:23–24 says, "'I have the right to do anything,' you say—but not everything is beneficial. 'I have the right to do anything'—but not everything is constructive. No one should seek their own good, but the good of others."

You might have told yourself that it doesn't matter what you do these days because there's always someone who will be offended, so you've decided just to live your life and not worry about what others think or believe about you. That attitude, Paul said, is a big part of the problem. That kind of thinking is wrong and harmful since it is void of a key component of a unified church: love. Our work for Christ is meaningless if our love for others is missing.

Giving up my rights to spare another Christian potential harm should not be seen as drudgery or dogmatism. It's the natural behavior of true love. David Platt echoed this thought: "We are settling for a Christianity that revolves around catering to ourselves when the central message of Christianity is actually about abandoning ourselves."[29]

Please understand that the apostle Paul was not insisting that we abandon our personal freedoms to the ignorant bias of every "spiritual" bigot. There is no need to do an exhaustive survey to make sure that no one is offended by the liberties we've chosen to exercise. Paul instructed us to consider the sincere believers right around us who are truly influenced by how we live out our Christian faith and affected by our spiritual example. We have different sizes and scopes to our influence.

Can people change the contents of their rights boxes? Of course. Sometimes people grow in ways that allow them to add freedoms that used to be off-limits for them. Sometimes when they grow, they subtract certain behaviors or liberties because they become convicted in their consciences and no longer feel freedom from God in those respects.

Here's what never changes: my rights from Christ are *always* less important than the faith of my brothers and sisters in Christ. It's never right to claim my rights at the expense of leading other Christians down the wrong road or causing them to doubt their personal walks with the Lord.

Rights and the Gospel

This leads to Paul's third principle: your knowledge and rights must be viewed through the lens of the gospel.

> *So this weak brother or sister, for whom Christ died, is destroyed by your knowledge. When you sin against them in this way and wound their weak conscience, you sin against Christ.*
>
> ***—1 Corinthians 8:11–12***

When I let my rights become more important than the life and walk of a person for whom Christ died, I've made myself and my rights more important than the work of

Christ and His cross. I've elevated my freedom above the gospel and limited my effectiveness in displaying Christ to the world around me. I've sinned not only against a fellow Christ-follower, but against Jesus Himself.

> *If your brother or sister is distressed because of what you eat, you are no longer acting in love. Do not by your eating destroy someone for whom Christ died. ... Do not destroy the work of God for the sake of food. All food is clean, but it is wrong for a person to eat anything that causes someone else to stumble.*
>
> **—*Romans 14:15, 20***

If I knowingly allow my personal freedom to destroy the faith of another Christ-follower, my freedom has been used by Satan as a weapon of mass destruction.

First Corinthians 8:13 says, "Therefore, if what I eat causes my brother or sister to fall into sin, I will never eat meat again, so that I will not cause them to fall." Paul presented a scenario for us to understand the role each of us plays in another Christian's life. Thankfully, this verse is not indicating that Paul became a vegetarian.

Most likely, Paul was using hyperbole, but his point was a powerful one: if my right or personal freedom to eat meat sacrificed to an idol causes another Christian I influence to stumble into sin and fall away from Christ, I will gladly go one step farther and never eat *any* meat again. Why? Because eliminating the meat altogether would be worth it for the sake of someone with whom I'm spending eternity. Consider this concept in the following examples:

1. If I know that watching a particular R-rated movie with certain Christian friends would violate their clean consciences and cause them to stumble in their faith, potentially leading them

away from intimacy with Christ, then I'd rather never watch another R-rated movie than violate my friends' spiritual walks, because my freedom to watch movies isn't worth it.

2. If I know that mowing my yard on a Sunday would deeply offend my Christian neighbor and cause a rift between us, then I'll gladly give up mowing on Sundays for as long as we're neighbors. Why? Because mowing on a Sunday isn't worth the cost. My freedom in Christ should edify others, not destroy them or our relationship.

Does this approach seem impossible to practice perfectly? Probably. Is it hyperbole? Likely so. Is there life-changing and church-strengthening truth here? Without a doubt. Paul highlighted this important Christ-like attitude so that we could understand it and implement it. The bottom line is that real freedom is not about me demanding my rights. Real freedom is knowing my rights and being willing to give them up for someone else's spiritual benefit. That's real freedom, and that's real love.

Jesus, of course, is our best example of this. He loved people more than His own liberties. He was willing to give up His exalted rights and even His earthly life for the greater good of others (Philippians 2:6–8). In light of His unparalleled sacrifice, we can surely give up any temporary freedoms that we know are hurting the faith of those Christ came to save.

Our love for Jesus is revealed in our love for one another. If you insist on exercising your personal freedoms while knowing full well that they are causing spiritual damage to the Christians closest to you, you're not really free, and you're not walking in love. The gospel must be the first priority. The gospel is greater than my rights.

Love always trumps liberty. My rights are subject to the gospel. What's going to matter fifty years from now, the freedom I can choose to exercise or the person whose life I can choose to influence?

If any of my rights hinder the work of the gospel in another Christian's life, I must gladly and lovingly refuse my right for the sake of the gospel and its deep work in the lives of the people I love. You see, the Corinthians were proud of their rights rather than being humble in them. A lack of humility leads to a lack of unity. That goes for our homes, small groups, workplaces, and churches. Pride divides, but humility unites. Jim Elliott was correct when he wrote in his diary, "He is no fool who gives what he cannot keep, to gain what he cannot lose."[30]

Let me emphasize this one last time: *we are our brothers' keepers*. How well are you doing in this area?

WORKBOOK

Chapter Three Questions

Question: Do you think that a pastor, missionary, or other church leader should have higher or stricter personal standards than the rest of the congregation? Why or why not? What scriptures support your viewpoint?

___

___

___

___

___

___

___

___

___

___

___

___

Question: What gray areas in the church today are potential stumbling blocks that could draw believers back into their old lives and lead them away from their new lives in Christ? Describe a time when you witnessed spiritual destruction in a weaker believer's life because others were more focused on their rights, liberties, or preferences than on edification and sanctification in the body of Christ.

____

____

____

____

____

____

____

____

____

____

____

____

Question: Describe a right that you have subtracted from your rights box as you have matured in Christ. What is a right that you have added as you have grown in your Christian walk? How did God change your heart and your thinking about these issues?

____

____

____

____

____

____

____

____

____

____

____

____

Action: Make a list of the things in your rights box. At the top, write "Love over Liberty." Consider which of these rights might be a stumbling block and to whom. Specify how you will limit your liberty out of love for the weaker believer so that you will experience the true freedom of loving like Christ.

Chapter Three Notes

CHAPTER FOUR

The Second Quandary: Weaker Believer Syndrome

Be careful, however, that the exercise of your rights does not become a stumbling block to the weak. ... When you sin against them in this way and wound their weak conscience, you sin against Christ. Therefore, if what I eat causes my brother or sister to fall into sin, I will never eat meat again, so that I will not cause them to fall.

—1 Corinthians 8:9, 12–13

There is an enormous difference between growing old in the Lord and growing up in Him. One is automatic and requires no effort at all ... just aging. But the other is never automatic, or easy. It calls for personal discipline, continual determination, and spiritual desire. Churches are full of sleepy saints who are merely "logging time" in God's family.[31]

—Chuck Swindoll

In his sermon titled "Left-Handed Power," Dr. Vic Pentz shared this fascinating story:[32]

Recently I heard the story of a ten-year-old boy in Hawaii who got in a car wreck and lost his left arm. After he recovered, he wanted to learn judo, which sort of confused his parents, but they figured, "What's the harm?" So they got him a judo instructor and the instructor said, "I want you to learn just one move; let's just work on this one move." So they worked on that one move for a long, long time. Eventually the teacher said, "Okay, you've almost got this move down; time to enter a competition." The boy said, "That's crazy. I can't win; I don't have a left arm and I only know one move—I'm gonna get creamed." The judo instructor said, "Well, let's see what happens."

So the boy entered a local competition, and he won the tournament in his age division. Afterwards, the boy said to his teacher, *"How is this possible? How did I win this tournament with only one move and no left arm?"* The teacher said, "It's easy. The one move you mastered is one of the hardest moves in judo and the only defense against it involves your opponent grabbing your left arm."

Weak or Strong: Who Is "Right"?

Determining who is weaker or stronger, physically or spiritually, is not always easy or obvious. One of the big problems in today's church is that many stronger Christians think that they are weaker, and many weaker believers think that they're stronger. This creates confusion regarding who in the church should be out front leading and who should sit back and learn.

The fact is that a church will never grow past the maturity level of its leaders. When a church's leadership is mostly made up of weaker believers, the church itself will be weaker. Weaker churches are more fragile and easily divided. Divided churches are ineffective at best and poisonous at worst. Discerning the difference between a stronger and a weaker believer is, therefore, of the utmost importance. The spiritual growth and gospel effectiveness of the church is at stake.

In the previous chapter, I introduced you to two teams: Team Meat and Team No Meat. Team Meat, whom Paul referred to as the stronger believers, reasoned, "False gods aren't gods. They're just statues of wood and stone. A non-existent god can't contaminate meat. If it's not real, it can't hurt you." The members of Team Meat based this perspective on their growing spiritual knowledge and understanding of truth. Because of their strong consciences, they understood that God had given them the right and the freedom to eat whatever they wanted.

On the other side, the members of Team No Meat, whom Paul referred to as the weaker believers, considered it a horrible sin to eat meat sacrificed to false gods. They had yet to know the full liberation of the gospel and enjoy all of the freedoms it provides. They understood that the Lord had graciously delivered them from their wicked past, and they dared not return to anything remotely resembling idolatry. According to them, neither should any other believers. They argued, "No one who claims Christ as Savior and Lord has the right to eat meat offered to an idol." Their weaker consciences were offended when other believers ate meat that they could never enjoy.

It's important to understand that both groups did what they did with the same motive: they wanted to honor God. They desperately desired to please Christ. It's not that the actions of one group were clearly right and the other wrong. The distinction between the two groups was spiritual maturity. Eating meat sacrificed to an idol was neither condemned nor condoned in Scripture. It was a disputable matter. Disputable matters are the gray areas. These are morally neutral things that aren't directly called sin in the Bible. Some people have the conviction that these things are wrong while others do not.

Charles Haddon Spurgeon, long considered the

greatest preacher of the nineteenth century, was reported as saying in one of his sermons, "Well, dear friends, you know that some men can do to the glory of God what to other men would be sin. And … I intend to smoke a good cigar to the glory of God before I go to bed to-night."[33] In our current culture, some Christians think that getting a tattoo is a sin while others see no problem with it. It's a disputable, non-moral matter. Paul didn't discourage discussion of disputable matters. Rather, he denounced division because of them. We are to converse about them without quarreling over them. But how do we do that?

One Goal: Faith

Paul's goal was for every member of the church to utilize the strength of his or her own spiritual knowledge and faith, combined with a deep love for others, to spread the gospel. Stronger doesn't mean better, and weaker doesn't mean inferior. Paul's words in 1 Corinthians 8 were not measuring value but spiritual maturity. Spiritual maturity is not about how much time you've put in but how much truth you've absorbed and applied.

The stronger believers had a greater grasp of spiritual truth, resulting in a greater maturity in their faith. The weaker believers, however, had less overall spiritual knowledge and understanding, and because of it, they had weaker faith.

Paul's command to the stronger believers was to grow in love so that they would be more patient with the weaker believers. His command to the weaker believers was to grow in knowledge of the truth so that they would become more mature like the stronger believers. When stronger believers grow in *love* and weaker believers grow in *truth*, the whole church grows in *unity*.

Paul refused to choose a side. Instead, he pointed them to the goal: faith. We need to focus on our faith, not our rights. As a person's faith gets stronger, these gray areas, these disputable matters, hold less and less power. The stronger your faith, the greater clarity you will have on the things that hold eternal value.

What strengthens our faith? The truth of God's Word is timeless: "...faith comes by hearing, and hearing by the word of God" (Romans 10:17 NKJV). The more we understand and follow God's Word, the stronger and wiser our faith becomes and the less dogmatic we become on disputable matters. As we mature in our faith, we become more flexible regarding the issues that divide Christians.

The strongest churches are full of people who refuse to divide over disputable freedoms and instead unite over undeniable truth. Each of us is called to do his or her part by growing in spiritual maturity and faith. This is accomplished by learning and living the Word of God.

The more rigid your rules about disputable matters, the weaker your faith. That's important to understand because we tend to think just the opposite. In the Corinthian church, one group said, "You can eat that meat or not eat that meat." The other group said, "No, there needs to be a firm rule that no one can eat that meat." Paul taught that those who need more rules about disputable matters are the weaker believers.

But how often do we get this backward in the church? We think that the people with the most rules, the people who condemn the most things and see sin in every little aspect of life, are the most disciplined and the most spiritual and have the strongest faith. Yet Paul said the opposite. He said that the faith of such individuals is so weak that things that aren't inherently sinful become sinful to them.

It is possible for churches to celebrate the very behavior that Paul called a symptom of weak faith. If we're not careful, we could push those around us toward the very type of life Paul called us to grow out of. I call this the *weaker believer syndrome.*

Weaker Believer Syndrome

It's been my experience that many churches inadvertently champion the weaker believer syndrome. They celebrate when people suffer from a type of "weaker believer fever." This is the idea that the more things you don't do, the more restrictions or rules you hold to, the better Christian you are. Because of that error in judgment, Christians have inherited a multitude of rules and traditions forbidding behaviors that the Bible doesn't even call sin. We are the ones who have formed and enforced these rules.

Getting rigid and dogmatic about neutral practices rapidly turns into protecting personal preferences. This is the essence of the weaker believer syndrome. Weaker believer fever burns hot in many churches today. To detect and discern it in order to avoid it, we must ask ourselves these questions:

- How do you know if you have the weaker believer syndrome?
- How can you test for weaker believer fever?
- How can you tell the difference between being disciplined, holy, and strong and being immature, legalistic, and weak in gospel understanding?

We need to challenge ourselves to be purposeful and introspective. Otherwise, we will continue to champion and celebrate weaker believers who become church leaders. Leaders who are weaker believers subsequently build churches that are inherently weak and easy to divide.

These churches enslave people by assigning them the exact contents for their rights boxes rather than leading them to freedom in Christ Jesus. In these inflexible, unbending churches, if you don't fall in line, you'll eventually get pushed out.

You might be a weaker believer if…

I want to give you four warning signs to help you recognize if you're struggling with the weaker believer syndrome.

Warning Sign #1: You are easily offended by the actions of others. First Corinthians 8:9 says, "Be careful, however, that the exercise of your rights does not become a stumbling block to the weak." A stumbling block is anything that negatively affects a person's spiritual growth.

Here we find an explicit command: the stronger believers are to be careful not to use their rights capriciously, causing weaker believers to stumble as they follow Jesus. Paul continued, "'I have the right to do anything,' you say—but not everything is beneficial. 'I have the right to do anything'—but not everything is constructive. No one should seek their own good, but the good of others" (1 Corinthians 10:23–24). Paul's clear point was that for Christians, personal freedom must be tempered by love toward other Christians, and even love should not be abused.

If we look closely, we also find an implicit command: the weaker believers are to be careful not to let the freedoms of others cause them to stumble. It's a two-way responsibility. Romans 14:3 says, "Let not the one who eats despise the one who abstains, and let not the one who abstains pass judgment on the one who eats…" (ESV).

Interestingly, every time the New Testament talks about a believer being offended by the non-sinful behavior of another believer, it's the weaker believer who is offended. When weaker believers see other believers engaging in a disputable matter they have deemed wrong for themselves, they allow the behavior of those believers to upset and offend them.

Ironically, the response of weaker believers to behaviors that aren't sinful can sometimes be sinful. They get offended because they believe that a certain behavior is ungodly, and then they act like the devil in response. Some of the most ungodly behavior I've ever witnessed has been from professed Christians who were responding to things they believed to be sin.

For instance, I believe that it's acceptable for a pastor like me to come to church dressed casually rather than wearing a suit or tie. I feel a freedom from God to dress casually for corporate worship. Years ago, a man was infuriated with me because of my Sunday attire. He angrily said, "Casual clothes on a pastor in church are disrespectful." On another occasion, he approached me at a funeral to which I wore a suit and tie. He looked at me disdainfully and commented, "You'll wear a suit and tie to honor the dead but not to honor God?"

Though he had been a member of the church for decades, he left within the first year of my arrival. He turned his dogmatic stance on a neutral practice into a demand on me. His personal preference or conviction wasn't just something to discuss between the two of us; he made it something that brought division. Eventually, my response became, "Please find for me the 'Pastor Dress Code' in the Bible. Whatever it says, I'll gladly follow."

Guess what? He didn't find it. You won't, either.

I tried to be loving and gracious with this man about it. I tried to help him understand how the formality of a suit and tie can be a major barrier to those who are already intimidated by being in church or speaking with a pastor. I did this with purpose and prayer. He refused to listen and wouldn't budge. He didn't care about how this issue impacted people attending our church looking for God, and he wasn't interested in church unity or personal spiritual growth. He allowed his personal stance to lead him into relational sin. He saw himself as the stronger believer helping the weaker believer get straightened out. And believe me, he wasn't gentle about it.

Likewise, we had a deacon who was known as captain of the hat patrol. Whenever he saw a young man with a hat on in church, he approached him with contempt, ripped the hat off of his head, chastised his obvious irreverence, and walked off self-righteously. He believed that he was acting on God's behalf. He was "protecting" the holiness of God's house based on his misinterpretation of 1 Corinthians 11:4: "Every man praying or prophesying, having his head covered, dishonors his head" (NKJV). The Bible does not condemn wearing a hat in church. It does, however, clearly condemn being unloving and unkind. We gently reminded the deacon of his call to represent God's grace in his position of leadership.

Theologian N.T. Wright stressed this same sentiment: "People who believe that Jesus is already Lord and that He will appear again as judge of the world are called and equipped (to put it mildly) to think and act quite differently in the world from those who don't."[34] If we're going to give the world something different, we must start by being different. First Peter 4:8 says, "Above all, love each other deeply, because love covers over a multitude of sins."

True love for others produces a desire to forgive their sin, help their spiritual growth, and limit the exposure of their missteps. Why? Because that's exactly what God has done for us. In Jesus, God offers grace and forgiveness to cover our sin and wash it away. He doesn't rub it in; He scrubs it out. When He lives in us, we want to do the same thing for others.

Warning Sign #2: Every issue seems "gospel-sized."

First Corinthians 8:8 states, "But food does not bring us near to God; we are no worse if we do not eat, and no better if we do." Paul was saying, "This shouldn't be a big deal. It doesn't matter what you eat or don't eat." However, he added a caveat:

> *Be careful, however, that the exercise of your rights does not become a stumbling block to the weak. For if someone with a weak conscience sees you, with all your knowledge, eating in an idol's temple, won't that person be emboldened to eat what is sacrificed to idols? So this weak brother or sister, for whom Christ died, is destroyed by your knowledge.*
>
> ***—1 Corinthians 8:9–11***

For weaker believers, everything is of equal importance. Consequently, disputable matters become as important as the gospel itself. Getting people to stop wearing hats in church becomes as important as getting people to believe that Jesus is the Savior of the world. Sadly, for some, being on hat patrol, suit duty, or meat surveillance becomes a greater passion than being a gospel witness.

Some people can't drink alcohol without feeling Satan pull them toward sinful behavior, so they can't imagine that anyone else can. Some can't have Santa Claus at Christmas without feeling that they have slighted Jesus' birth and the real meaning of Christmas, so they don't believe that anyone else can. Some just can't worship wholeheartedly with drums in the worship band, so they assume that everyone else is negatively affected as well.

For the weaker believer, personal convictions, personal preferences, and direct biblical commands all run together. They all carry the same weight of importance. Everything is a big deal. If a weaker believer disagrees with anything, it becomes a matter of spiritual life and death.

As you can imagine, it's rather difficult for weaker believers to be happy in *any* local church. In fact, being in church is downright stressful for them because every little thing they disagree with is a catastrophic threat to the very life and purity of the church as a whole. They feel compelled to shine the light and right the wrong. When everything is a matter of right and wrong, then everything is as important as the gospel.

No wonder many church members find themselves in constant conflict with nearly everyone on some level. If everything becomes the gospel for you, then you are close to having no gospel at all. The gospel is God's grace alone through faith alone in Jesus alone. If you're attaching anything else to the gospel, then that's not grace alone, that's not faith alone, and that's not Jesus alone. And that is not the gospel.

In other words, if everything is as big a deal as the gospel, then the gospel isn't really a big deal. The inevitable result is a dilution and distortion of the wondrous gospel of Jesus Christ. Stronger believers, according to Paul, refuse to make every right and freedom a gospel-sized issue.

Warning Sign #3: You insist that everyone agree with your personal convictions. Remember, weaker believers in the early church weren't content simply to follow their convictions and abstain from eating meat that had been sacrificed to idols. They wanted to impose their convictions on everyone else by demanding that other believers were not to eat meat, either. They said, "If I can't, then you can't. If it's wrong for me, then it's wrong for you." Weaker believers only feel comfortable around people whose rights boxes look a lot like their own.

This has been and continues to be a major source of friction and division in the church. Dissension occurs when Christians turn their personal, spiritual *preferences* into eternal, spiritual *principles* for everyone. Fighting over personal preferences, not biblical principles, has damaged thousands of American churches over the last one hundred years.

Romans 14:1–4 (emphasis added) speaks directly to this very issue:

> *Accept the one whose faith is weak, without quarreling over* ***disputable matters****. One person's faith allows them to eat anything, but another, whose faith is weak, eats only vegetables. The one who eats everything must not treat with contempt the one who does not, and the one who does not eat everything must not judge the one who does, for God has accepted them. Who are you to judge someone else's servant? To their own master, servants stand or fall. And they will stand, for the Lord is able to make them stand.*

Stronger believers who feel God's freedom in some morally neutral matters are not to look with contempt on weaker believers. Likewise, weaker believers are not to look down on other believers by being judgmental. What is to be our response to each other when we disagree on the contents of our rights boxes? *Acceptance of one another.*

Our response shouldn't be to convert one another to our personal views. We shouldn't shun one another until someone concedes. We shouldn't separate from each other and find new church homes. The right response is to accept one another like God has accepted us: lovingly, graciously, patiently, and unconditionally.

Disputable matters within the church should lead to dialogue, not division. We need to discuss the issues. We might debate them. We may even disagree on them. But we must not divide over them.

Warning Sign #4: Your primary focus is on external, superficial matters. For the weaker Corinthian believers, external action was what mattered—what they ate or didn't eat. Paul, however, said that what really mattered was *why* they did or did not eat the meat, contending that it was all about the internal motive, not the external action.

If the reason they didn't eat the meat was that they had weak faith, that was wrong and needed to be corrected. However, if the reason they didn't eat was out of love for other believers who were struggling, that would be justified. If the reason they ate the meat was that they were selfish and didn't care about anyone else, that was wrong. If the reason they ate it was that they were learning to trust the gospel more, then that would be warranted. Do you see where I'm going here?

Why the Corinthian Christians did what they did mattered even more than what they did. We can do the right thing with the wrong motive and still be wrong, because the intentions of our hearts matter. Believers with a weaker faith tend to focus on behavior rather than motive because behavior is easier to measure and often easier to control.

The gospel isn't chiefly focused on changing our *behavior* but changing our *identity*. The goal of the gospel is not just to get us to behave a certain way—to stop drinking, lying, or sleeping around. People can get sober, be honest, and remain chaste and still go to hell.

The goal of the gospel is that we will trust in the saving work of Jesus Christ, be united to Him through faith, and be washed, reconciled, and justified. Our entire identity changes, and then our behavior changes as a result, not the other way around. We must get the order right, because one is the gospel and the other is not. A new identity gives us new behavior, not the other way around.

It's not "clean up, then come to Jesus." When we come to Jesus by faith and believe what He has done for us on the cross and through His resurrection, He saves us. Then, because He is in us, He begins to change us. Gradually He will make us more and more like Him. When our identity changes, so will our behavior.

What if I'm the "weaker believer"?

I'm sure we can all say that we struggle with our behaviors and our hearts. Would you confess that you've thought of yourself as a stronger believer when, in fact, you are not? Most importantly, do you know why you're stuck in the weaker believer way of living? Why do you allow yourself to be dogmatic, even offensive, about disputable matters? If you fall into the weaker believer way of living, allow God's Word to challenge you to become a stronger believer. Never forget that rules can change a person's behavior, but only God can change a person's heart.

In his admonition, Paul diagnosed the problem, but he also provided the cure: "But food does not bring us near to God; we are no worse if we do not eat, and no better if we do" (1 Corinthians 8:8). Food will not make you right with God. Only one thing, only one Person, can make you right with God, and that is Jesus Christ, through His gospel. This is the only way for us to be brought close to and made right with God the Father: "We are made right with God by placing our faith in Jesus Christ. And this is true for everyone who believes, no matter who we are" (Romans 3:22 NLT).

The only cure for weaker believer syndrome is Jesus. Attending church will not make you right with God. Giving generously to missions will not make you right with God. Serving in church will not make you right with God. Reading your Bible and praying every day will not make you right with God. Not having sex before or outside of marriage will not make you right with God. These are the actions of Christians who have embraced the gospel and chosen to let their hearts and then their behavior display God's glory.

The fact is that if you trust any of those things to make you right with God, you won't be right with God. Only Jesus and His gospel can get the job done. As your faith in Jesus grows and becomes stronger, He sets you free from the external, superficial works you were trusting to help you be close to God. As your faith in Him grows, your trust in His grace grows. You slowly move from the No Meat Team to the Meat Team.

Again, it's not inherently wrong to be a weaker believer. It's just wrong if you're content to stay one. Do you believe with your whole heart in Jesus? Have you fully surrendered to Him? Have you personally repented of your sins—those things the Lord calls sin—and do you believe that your only hope of heaven is in His life, death, and resurrection? Are you growing in the truth and wanting to trust Him more? Are you growing out of a life of rules and growing into a life of faith? May the Lord cure all of us of the weaker believer syndrome by helping us to grow in the grace of His gospel.

Unity Because of Love

The weaker are to grow in truth, and the stronger are to grow in love, so the whole church grows in unity. Unity in the church doesn't happen on its own. It requires obedience from all of us—obedience to God's command to love others and honor them above ourselves. If I know that some of my rights damage your faith, I should willingly sacrifice my freedom for the benefit of your faith because of love.

Charles Spurgeon, the famous cigar-smoking pastor mentioned earlier, was walking down the street at the height of his fame and saw a sign which read, "We sell the cigar that Charles Spurgeon smokes." After reading this sign, Spurgeon gave up the habit. He came to understand that his freedom might cause others to stumble.[35]

You see, it's not just figuring out for myself if I can participate in these neutral matters without my faith being negatively impacted. I also need to be cognizant of how those actions might affect the believers around me. My freedom isn't more important than others' faith. Love trumps my rights. Love limits my liberties.

What does God's love look like?

> *But God demonstrates his own love for us in this: While we were still sinners, Christ died for us.*
>
> ***—Romans 5:8***

> *Let this mind be in you which was also in Christ Jesus, who, being in the form of God, did not consider it robbery to be equal with God, but made Himself of no reputation, taking the form of a bondservant, and coming in the likeness of men. And being found in appearance as a man, He humbled Himself and became obedient to the point of death, even the death of the cross.*
>
> ***—Philippians 2:5–8** (NKJV)*

> *For God so loved the world that He gave His only begotten Son, that whoever believes in Him should not perish but have everlasting life.*
>
> ***—John 3:16** (NKJV)*

These verses demonstrate that God's love for us is most vividly seen in His willingness to sacrifice for us. He wasn't obligated to save us. He didn't have to forge a way to forgive us. Jesus wasn't forced out of heaven to take on human flesh. He didn't have to die on a cross. He chose to do these things. He had the complete freedom and right to stay in heaven and let us perish in our cesspool of sin. He would have been perfectly justified in doing so because of

His own rights, but the love of God trumped the liberty of God. Christ sacrificed His freedoms so that we could be free.

Similarly, we demonstrate genuine, godly love through our willing sacrifices for others. I'm to love you more than my freedoms. I'm to love the gospel more than my rights. What I'm willing to give and give up for the benefit of others is a great indication of my level of love.

I don't know the source of this story, but the truth of it hasn't escaped me. During the Christmas holidays, a man parked his car near a convenience store to pick up the morning newspaper. As he came out of the store, he noticed a dirty, disheveled little boy looking at his car. With his paper under his arm, the man opened the car door to get inside.

"Mister," the boy blurted out, "how much would a new car like this cost?"

The man responded, "I really don't know. My brother gave me this car as a gift last Christmas."

The ragged little boy looked unbelievingly at the car with a look of wonder in his eyes and said something unexpected. He didn't say, "Gee, I wish I could get a car like that." He said, "Gee, I wish I could be a brother like that."

You can sacrifice without love, but you cannot love without sacrifice. When God's love grips you, giving up something for the sake of someone else doesn't even feel like a sacrifice. It feels like a privilege.

WORKBOOK

Chapter Four Questions

Question: Do you consider yourself a weaker believer or a stronger believer? Why? Would you say that most of your church leadership is made up of weaker or stronger Christians? Are there changes that need to be made in how you choose, evaluate, and train leaders in your church?

___

___

___

___

___

___

___

___

___

___

___

Question: As a church leader, do you regularly choose sides on gray areas and disputable matters, or do you point your congregation toward faith and a greater knowledge of God's Word? What is the difference in pastoral leadership when the pastor takes sides instead of teaching faith?

____

____

____

____

____

____

____

____

____

____

____

____

Question: Take a look at the four-pronged test for weaker believer syndrome:

- You are easily offended by the actions of others.
- Every issue seems gospel-sized.
- Everyone must agree with your personal convictions.
- External, superficial matters are your primary focus.

How do those traits line up with your current level of faith? Consider your responses to the disputes, gray areas, and rights that you listed in your answers to the workbook questions in Chapter Three. What is the motivation behind each of your decisions? What is your attitude toward those whose decisions are different from yours?

____

____

____

____

____

____

____

____

____

____

____

____

Action: When stronger believers grow in love and weaker believers grow in truth, the whole church grows in unity. Write out an action plan for your church to help facilitate this growth. Actions might include specific messages, times of directed fellowship to help stronger and weaker believers better understand and appreciate each other's perspectives, personal testimonies from believers who are growing in maturity and Christ-likeness, and re-evaluation of areas of ministry that focus primarily on rules and appearances.

Chapter Four Notes

CHAPTER FIVE

The Answer: For the Love of the Gospel

If others have this right of support from you, shouldn't we have it all the more? But we did not use this right. On the contrary, we put up with anything ***rather than hinder the gospel of Christ****.*

—1 Corinthians 9:12 ***(emphasis added)***

The Gospel is not how people get to heaven. The Gospel is how people get to God.[36]

—John Piper

There's a famous story about a group of soldiers during World War II who had lost a friend in battle and wanted to bury him with honor.[37] They found a graveyard behind a church; a white fence surrounded it. When they found the priest, they asked if they could bury their friend in the graveyard. This was the exchange:

"Was he Catholic?" the priest inquired.

"No, he was not," answered the soldiers.

"I'm sorry, then," said the priest. "Our graveyard is reserved for members of the holy church. But you can bury your friend outside the fence. I will see that the gravesite is cared for."

"Thank you, Father," said the soldiers, and they proceeded to bury their friend just outside the graveyard, on the other side of the fence.

When the war ended, the soldiers decided to visit the gravesite of their friend before returning home. They remembered the location of the church and the grave, just outside the fence. They searched for it but couldn't find it. Finally, they went to the priest to inquire about its location.

"Sir, we cannot find our friend's grave."

"Well," answered the priest, "after you buried your fallen friend, it just didn't seem right to me that he should be buried outside the fence."

"So, you moved his grave?" asked the soldiers.

"No," said the priest. "I moved the fence."

None of us deserves a place "inside the fence" of God's forever family. But God acted in love and grace toward us by providing Jesus as an atoning sacrifice for our sins and the source of eternal life. In a sense, God "moved the fence" and brought us to Himself by His own will and good pleasure. Solely because of Christ—not because of any glorious works or inherent righteousness of our own—we have gone from outsiders to insiders in the Kingdom of God. This is the wonderful news of the gospel.

When the gospel of Jesus is our framework and filter for how we treat others, we will find love, patience, sacrifice, and compassion much easier. It is to this passionate love for the gospel that Paul pointed the Corinthians.

Paul: A Case Study

Paul knew that the Corinthians would have difficulty accepting his reply to their question without a mind-changing and heart-stirring example, so he demonstrated how this principle of love over freedom works by pointing to his own life and ministry.

Paul had been their pastor for eighteen months before he moved on to plant other churches (Acts 18:11). While serving the Corinthian church, he was a bi-vocational pastor, functioning as both a pastor overseeing multiple ministries and a layman working with his hands. A bi-vocational pastor is one who, "either out of necessity or intentionality, works as both the pastor of a local church and in the secular marketplace."[38]

Paul was a pastor by day and a tentmaker by night. When he addressed the Christians in 1 Corinthians 9, he wanted them to understand that even though he did have the right or freedom to ask them to support his ministry full time, he chose to work as a tentmaker. He refused to exercise that freedom because he wanted what was best for them, even though what was best for them wasn't what was easiest for him.

In the same way that stronger believers today come alongside pastors and teachers to assist with ministry duties or help financially, Paul willingly sacrificed his time and finances to share the gospel and minister to the Corinthians. He chose to minister to the people even though that meant he had to spend additional time working for wages. Paul could have requested payment, but fortunately, God used stronger believers to pick up some of the slack.

Paul's "Right"

In this passage, Paul gave four clear reasons why it was within his God-given right to be paid for ministry.

Reason #1: His Apostolic Work

In 1 Corinthians 9:1, Paul asked, "Am I not free?" The Corinthians were saying, "We're free in Christ to do what we want. We can eat meat offered to idols. We can visit the pagan temples for social events. We don't have to do what they do, but we can still eat their food. We've been liberated by Christ."

Paul responded by directing the same question toward himself:

> *Am I not free? Am I not an apostle? Have I not seen Jesus our Lord? Are you not the result of my work in the Lord? Even though I may not be an apostle to others, surely I am to you! For you are the seal of my apostleship in the Lord.*
> ***—1 Corinthians 9:1–2***

Essentially, Paul asked the Corinthians if he was not also free to take advantage of his rights.

None of the Corinthians could have argued with any of Paul's points. He basically told them, "You know who I am. You know what I've done for you. You know the work I've put in. You know that Christ used me to reveal the gospel to you. You know you're not going to hell because Jesus sent me on a rescue mission for you. Think about all the work and blessings you've received through my work for you. Didn't I have a right to be paid for it?" The answer to this question would be a resounding "yes!"

Reason #2: Common Sense

Pastors and Christian leaders like the apostle Paul nurture and continually attend to our spiritual needs, which is even more reason to support them in their ministry. Paul posed the following questions:

> *Don't we have the right to food and drink? Don't we have the right to take a believing wife along with us, as do the other apostles and the Lord's brothers and Cephas? Or is it only I and Barnabas who lack the right to not work for a living?*
>
> **—1 Corinthians 9:4–6**

He was saying, "Not only do all the other apostles get paid for their spiritual ministry, but they even have wives and families that are supported financially by the church. Can all the other pastors and apostles receive a salary from gospel ministry, but not Barnabas and me?" Clearly, the answer was "no."

Reason #3: The Bible's Command

Paul moved from human reasoning to God's Word:

> *Do I say this merely on human authority? Doesn't the Law say the same thing? For it is written in the Law of Moses: "Do not muzzle an ox while it is treading out the grain." Is it about oxen that God is concerned? Surely he says this for us, doesn't he? Yes, this was written for us, because whoever plows and threshes should be able to do so in the hope of sharing in the harvest. If we have sown spiritual seed among you, is it too much if we reap a material harvest from you? If others have this right of support from you, shouldn't we have it all the more?*
>
> **—1 Corinthians 9:8–12a**

Paul quoted Deuteronomy 25:4, speaking about muzzling the ox treading grain, to support his claim. You may be asking yourself, "What do an ox and grain have to do with ministry and individual rights?" In those days, farmers put the grain on a threshing floor or a large, open area and strapped a heavy, round stone to an ox. The ox walked around and around for hours, dragging that large stone, which crushed the grain so that the kernels came out of their husks.

God commanded His people not to put a muzzle on the ox's mouth, which would have prevented him from bending down occasionally to eat a mouthful of the grain he was threshing. Muzzling the ox would be unjust and inhumane. The ox was doing the work, so he should be able to eat of his labor. Paul used this as a metaphor to explain that spiritual workers are entitled to compensation for their labor.

As an adult, I've had jobs in the church and outside of the church. Based on my experience, I can report that ministry is tough! So, while pastors serve the church like oxen stomping on the grain for their congregations, don't muzzle them and prevent them from partaking of what is being produced. As you receive spiritual blessings, it is right to supply material benefits.

Reason #4: The Words of Jesus

> *Don't you know that those who serve in the temple get their food from the temple, and that those who serve at the altar share in what is offered on the altar? In the same way, **the Lord** has commanded that those who preach the gospel should receive their living from the gospel.*
>
> ***—1 Corinthians 9:13–14*** *(emphasis added)*

Jesus commanded the church to support its ministers.

Choosing to dedicate your life to the work of the ministry means that you live off of the increase that comes from that work.

Paul reminded the Corinthians of what Jesus said in Luke 10 and Matthew 10: the church should provide financially for its leaders, who devote their lives to proclaiming the gospel. The New Testament clearly teaches the church that as we receive spiritual blessings from our church leaders, we should, in turn, share material blessings with them.

I would be remiss if I didn't take a moment to honor the church for which I pastor. They provide so phenomenally for me that it has given me the liberty to focus full-time on preaching and teaching the Word of God. My church is by far the most generous, most giving church I've ever served or encountered. At times, it's almost embarrassing how good they are to me. I know that my family and I are completely cared for not only spiritually, but also financially. For this, I am immensely thankful. Our church is a living testimony of faithful obedience to the Word of God.

Paul's Refusal

First Corinthians 8 is Paul's "do as I say" chapter, but 1 Corinthians 9 is Paul's "do as I do" chapter. He didn't just tell the Corinthians to love each other more than they loved their rights. He told them to look at his life and follow his example.

Paul devoted the first fourteen verses of 1 Corinthians 9 to explaining that he had every right and freedom to be paid as a gospel preacher when he was with the people of Corinth. However, he refused to exercise that right, willingly surrendering that freedom.

A Potential Problem

Paul wrote, "But we did not use this right. On the contrary, we put up with anything rather than *hinder* the gospel of Christ" (1 Corinthians 9:12b, emphasis added). Paul explained that we should be ready to deny ourselves just as he did so that nothing will hinder the progress of the gospel in us or through us.

That word *hinder* is interesting. In the Greek, it's *enkope*.[39] It means to halt or obstruct. Its root word, *egkopto*, can mean to cut off or chop up.[40] These words were sometimes used in a military sense, such as describing an army breaking up a road to keep an enemy from using it. Paul was largely saying, "I don't want to do anything that might hinder, obstruct, or chop up the roads that would lead you to Jesus. If getting paid would block up the road for people to be saved, then I'd rather work night and day to support myself. I'll put up with anything before I let that happen."

Let's consider his answer for a moment. Why would it have been an obstacle or hindrance to the gospel work if Paul received a salary? In that day, Greek cities were full of all kinds of itinerant teachers and preachers of various philosophies. Most were simply out to make money. They buzzed into town, taught their stuff, fleeced the people, and moved on when the money ran out.

Paul wanted to be drastically different from those teachers. He wanted it to be clear that no one had to pay to receive the gospel. What he had was free for everyone, and he was so intent on everyone else experiencing it that he supported himself in order to share the gospel with as many people as possible.

A Sacrificial Solution

While the gospel was free for everyone to receive, it

cost Paul a lot to get it to the people. However, he gladly did what needed to be done for the sake of others' souls. But Paul still needed to eat. So how did he survive?

Paul did two things. He went bi-vocational. He also had other churches that were more spiritually mature supporting him financially while he was working as a missionary to Corinth. Paul wrote, "I robbed other churches by receiving support from them so as to serve you" (2 Corinthians 11:8). The word *robbed*, of course, is hyperbole. The stronger gave so that the weaker wouldn't need to give.

Paul wasn't opposed to being paid to preach, but if it prevented people from accepting the gospel or otherwise hindered his gospel work, he didn't want payment. In those specific situations, he refused payment. Paul refused to let money be an obstacle to the spread of the gospel in Corinth.

This is true today of missionaries all over the world who are financially supported by their "sending" churches year after year. Countless churches send and sponsor missionaries to do gospel work in other locations. When you give to their local church, it has an international impact.

Our giving happens within our church, but the effect of that generosity goes beyond our home church into the rest of the world. God has blessed us incredibly so that we might be an incredible blessing to others in their gospel work. I praise God that we get to invest in the work of the gospel by following Paul's example in Scripture. All of us are called to follow Christ's mandate for the church to take responsibility for those who minister the Word.

Paul was not angry with the church for not compensating him for this work. Rather, his calling to preach the gospel without compensation was a sacrifice he freely embraced. He went on to say:

> *But I have not used any of these rights. And I am not writing this in the hope that you will do such things for me, for I would rather die than allow anyone to deprive me of this boast.*
>
> ***—1 Corinthians 9:15***

Paul said that he'd rather be dead than be confused with someone who only preached the gospel for a paycheck. Paul was not in ministry for the money but for the Messiah. His focus wasn't on what he could get from preaching the gospel but on what others would get by hearing and believing it.

However, Paul's amazing attitude toward personal sacrifice didn't end there.

A Duty to the Gospel

Paul continued:

> *For when I preach the gospel, I cannot boast, since I am compelled to preach. Woe to me if I do not preach the gospel!*
>
> ***—1 Corinthians 9:16***

What did Paul mean here? He meant that Jesus created him, called him, and then compelled him to preach the gospel. There was nothing else Paul could do or desired to do. It was not a freedom or a right but a duty. He didn't have the freedom *not* to preach. That word *woe* refers to the discipline of God. He knew that if he didn't preach the gospel, God would not let him off the hook, and there would be no joy in his life.

For Paul, preaching the gospel wasn't a sacrifice he gave to the Lord; it was his service. And his service was required:

> *If I preach voluntarily, I have a reward; if not voluntarily, I am simply discharging the trust committed to me. What then is my reward? Just this: that in preaching the gospel I may offer it free of charge, and so not make full use of my rights as a preacher of the gospel.*
>
> ***—1 Corinthians 9:17–18***

Paul had to preach. He was mandated by God to do so. Refusing to proclaim the Good News would have been sin for him. When he preached, he was doing what he was commanded to do. It was, therefore, not a sacrifice for him, but simple obedience. So how could Paul demonstrate how much he loved Christ, the gospel, and those he pastored? He did something he did not *have* to do. He preached the gospel for free. He had to preach the gospel, but he didn't have to preach it without financial support. Going above what was asked of him was his loving sacrifice to other saints and to his Savior.

Godly love is most genuinely demonstrated through willing sacrifice. Sharing the gospel was both Paul's willing sacrifice and his rich reward. This was the lesson he wanted the Corinthian Christians to grasp when it came to running the "race" of their salvation (1 Corinthians 9:24).

Preaching the gospel for free was Paul's reward because it allowed him to sacrifice his right for the love of the gospel. His reward was not that he got something *from* the gospel. His reward was that he got to give something *for* the gospel. R.C. Sproul, a noted and well-respected theologian, eloquently stated:[41]

> We do not segment our lives, giving some time to God, some to our business or schooling, while keeping parts to ourselves. The idea is to live all of our lives in the presence of God, under the authority of God, and for the honor and glory of God. That is what the Christian life is all about.

Paul's wholehearted love for the gospel and his experience of its life-changing power compelled him to sacrifice whatever was necessary for others to possess what he possessed.

What Is Your Sacrifice?

Imagine that you're sitting at home one evening when your doorbell rings. You answer the door, and two Secret Service agents are standing there. One of them says, "I'm sorry to bother you tonight, but the President of the United States has asked for you to come to the White House. He heard that you make the best pineapple upside-down cake in the whole country, and because that's his favorite, he wants you to come and make him one." You're honored and excited, and you agree to go.

You make your pineapple upside-down cake for the President. He eats it and loves it. Before you leave, he says, "That was incredible. I'd like to pay you for all your expenses, efforts, and inconveniences."

You respond, "No, Mr. President, you don't owe me anything. It's a privilege to get to come to the White House and bake for you. Just doing this for you is a huge reward for me." You don't do it *for* the reward. Doing it *is* the reward.

It gave Paul joy to give something for the gospel because the gospel was that valuable to him. Is this true for you? If godly love is most genuinely demonstrated through willing sacrifice, what are you joyfully sacrificing? What right or freedom are you surrendering for the benefit of the church and the love of the gospel? Is there any sacrifice of money, time, energy, privilege, or sleep that you make above anything required or expected simply because you rejoice in the gospel and want others to have it?

Oswald Chambers once said:[42]

> If we are willing to give up only wrong things for Jesus, never let us talk about being in love with Him. Anyone will give up wrong things if he knows how, but are we prepared to give up the best we have for Jesus Christ? The only right a Christian has is the right to give up his rights.

Again, you can sacrifice without love, but you cannot love without sacrifice. Whether it be by compassionately reaching out to others, tirelessly serving in ministry, earnestly interceding for those in need, or graciously providing financial assistance, may we all, like Paul, find a way to sacrifice willingly for the love of the gospel.

WORKBOOK

Chapter Five Questions

Question: What are some things that modern-day pastors and Christian workers do that might be obstacles to others receiving the gospel? What rights or freedoms have you sacrificed for the sake of the advancement of the gospel? Is your sacrifice made joyfully out of love or begrudgingly out of obligation?

____

____

____

____

____

____

____

____

____

____

____

____

Question: How is your church financially supporting missions? Is your congregation aware of the connection between their financial support and an unhindered ministry for the missionaries in the field? How can you encourage financial sacrifice from your congregation through communicating the physical and relational sacrifices of missionaries in the field?

____

____

____

____

____

____

____

____

____

____

____

____

Question: Reread the quote from Oswald Chambers: "If we are willing to give up only wrong things for Jesus, never let us talk about being in love with Him. Anyone will give up wrong things if he knows how, but are we prepared to give up the best we have for Jesus Christ? The only right a Christian has is the right to give up his rights." What is an area of your best that you can give to Christ? What is holding you back from making this sacrifice? How would your life look different if you began intentionally to sacrifice your rights for the advancement of the gospel?

____

____

____

____

____

____

____

____

____

____

____

____

Action: Read a memoir or biography of a Christian who made great sacrifices for the sake of the gospel (suggestions: Amy Carmichael, Dietrich Bonhoeffer, Hudson Taylor, Jim and Elisabeth Elliot). Especially take note of their attitudes in regard to those sacrifices. What perspective enabled them to surrender their rights joyfully?

Chapter Five Notes

CHAPTER SIX

The Cost: Whatever It Takes

Though I am free and belong to no one, I have made myself a slave to everyone, to win as many as possible.

—1 Corinthians 9:19

Our responsibility is to get God's Word to their ears. Only God can get the Word from their ears to their heart.[43]

—Albert Mohler

Michael Jordan is widely considered to be the greatest basketball player of all time. Stories of his competitive nature are legendary. Here is a small compilation from some notable sources:

Mike will compete with anything, though. If we're drinking water, Mike will be like, "I'll race you!"[44]

—Will Smith, actor

Michael lost to Dream Team coach Chuck Daly in a round of golf in Monte Carlo. Early the next morning, Jordan pounded on Daly's hotel door until Daly finally agreed to go play him again. Jordan won.[45]

—Rick Reilly, *Sports Illustrated* writer

Michael told Nick Anderson exactly what he was going to do to him on the court, then proceeded to do it. He said: "I'm coming down. I'm going to dribble it between my legs twice. I'm going to pump fake, and then I'm going to shoot a jumper. And then I'm going to look at you." And that's exactly what he did.[46]

—Shaquille O'Neal, former NBA player

During a game of golf, MJ shamed President Bill Clinton from the shorter white tees by saying, "You're going to play from the little girl's tees?"[47]

—The Wall Street Journal

There's a famous gambling story about Michael Jordan. ... Back before NBA teams had grasped the rejuvenating power of chartered airplanes, the Bulls were waiting for their luggage in Portland when Jordan slapped a hunny (a hundred dollar bill) on the conveyor belt: "I bet you my bags come out first." Jumping on the incredibly favorable odds, nine teammates happily accepted the wager. Sure enough, Jordan's bags led the rollout. He cackled with delight as he collected everyone's money. What none of the "suckers" knew, and what MJ never told them, was that he had bribed a baggage handler to help him out.[48]

—Bill Simmons, sportswriter

Michael Jordan's off-court sportsmanship and ethics were certainly questionable, but his primary mission was not. He was all about one thing: winning. Nothing else mattered. If you had asked Michael Jordan what he was willing to do to win, he probably would have said, "Whatever it takes."

The apostle Paul had that same vigor and mindset. His primary purpose was winning—not bets or basketball games, but unsaved people. His singular mission was winning people to Jesus Christ with the gospel. If you could have asked Paul what he would do to win people to Christ, I'm confident that he would have said the same thing: "Whatever it takes."

Paul's Winning Attitude

Call it passion, zeal, a fire, or even an obsession. Paul's main focus and concern was to devote every second of his day, every thought in his mind, and every ounce of his strength to bringing the gospel to people so they could escape God's wrath, be forgiven of their sin, and be reconciled to God through Jesus' cross and resurrection.

That's what Paul detailed for us in 1 Corinthians 9:19–23. Paul unequivocally proclaimed that he was willing to do anything, go anywhere, pay any price, endure any cost, make any sacrifice, and give up anything to win anyone at any time to Jesus Christ as long as it didn't compromise biblical principles or alter the gospel. His driving purpose and passion was to help rescue people headed to hell.

Would you say that you have that attitude and mindset? You might wonder if you even should have it. Maybe you figure that Paul felt this way because he was an apostle, so of course he did whatever it took. That was *his* job and *his* calling, not yours.

Paul challenged us to think bigger than this:

> *...For I am not seeking my own good but the good of many, so that they may be saved. Follow my example, as I follow the example of Christ.*
>
> ***—1 Corinthians 10:33–11:1***

Another translation says, "Imitate me, just as I also imitate Christ" (1 Corinthians 11:1 NKJV). To *imitate* means "to follow as a pattern, model, or example."[49] Did Jesus have a "whatever it takes" approach to saving people? Definitely! He left the perfection of heaven and the continuous worship of countless angels to be despised and nailed to a cross for the salvation of those who would repent and believe.

Paul's logic was this: "I'm imitating Jesus, who exemplified a 'whatever it takes' attitude to winning people to Himself. Now, as I'm imitating Jesus, you imitate me. If I'm doing what Jesus did and you are doing what I'm doing, you are also doing the same thing as Jesus."

Whatever It Takes

The internet can make you famous. Investments can make you rich. Politics can make you powerful. Professors can make you smart. Doctors can make you well. But only the gospel can make you right with God. It is our supreme honor to share this truth humbly with the people we encounter. Doing whatever it takes to see people saved by Christ and growing in His likeness isn't just for "professional" Christians like pastors and missionaries. It is for everyone who claims Christ as King.

Assess your attitude and lifestyle for a moment. Are you a "whatever it takes" kind of Christian? Let's find out. Take a look at these four characteristics that describe people who go all out for the sake of the gospel. How many of these characteristics describe you?

Characteristic #1: They waive their rights in order to win the lost.

Paul wrote, "Though I am free and belong to no one, I have made myself a slave to everyone, to win as many as possible" (1 Corinthians 9:19). At this point in his letter, Paul had extensively discussed freedoms and rights. He had explained that he was free to eat meat that had been sacrificed to idols and that he was free to receive a salary for preaching the gospel. But Paul also said that he was willing to waive those rights and freedoms if they hindered the mission.

Paul was willing to sacrifice anything and everything in his life if it meant that he could win more people to Christ. We are not free to live however we want and let the world go to hell. Our love for others must supersede our personal freedoms. Paul's purpose for waiving his rights was to win as many souls as possible. He didn't do it to be revered, respected, or rewarded. He did it so that others could be redeemed and reconciled to God.

Paul was what old-timers call a soul-winner. Some Christians don't like that term. I've even heard some say, "It's not our job to win the lost." And yet, did you notice how many times Paul used the word *win*? He said it five times in four verses:

- "…to win as many as possible" (1 Corinthians 9:19)
- "…to win the Jews" (1 Corinthians 9:20)
- "…to win those under the law" (1 Corinthians 9:20)
- "…to win those not having the law" (1 Corinthians 9:21)
- "…to win the weak" (1 Corinthians 9:22).

Paul knew the purpose for which he was alive and stayed focused on it. How are you doing right now with that? Speaking from experience, it's easy to get off track.

A pastor took his family on a cross-country road trip to Yellowstone National Park. To pass the time, they tried to spot license plates from all fifty states. By the time they got to Yellowstone, they had found about half of the states. Since Yellowstone is such a big tourist destination, they quickly found several more once they entered the park.

Larry, the youngest son, became almost obsessed with spotting all fifty states. Everywhere they stopped in Yellowstone, Larry combed the parking lots, looking at the license plates of all of the cars. He didn't even look at the attractions and scenic views because he didn't want to risk missing a new car that might pull into the lot.

Finally, one night as the family was eating dinner in a cafeteria near Yellowstone Falls, Larry burst into the restaurant, shouting, "Come here! Come here! You've got to see it! You won't believe it if you don't see it!" The whole family ran out to the parking lot, only to find that Larry was pointing at a blue Volkswagen with a Delaware license plate. It was the last of the fifty states that he needed to find. Larry even had them take his picture by the license plate to mark the grand occasion.

His pastor dad ended the story by saying, "Even now, a decade later, when we look at our Yellowstone pictures, that picture tells more about what Larry did in Yellowstone than anything else."

You see, Larry got it all backward. The license plate game was just supposed to entertain him during the trip; the real attractions were in Yellowstone. But Larry got so caught up in the distraction that he missed the attraction.

Paul, unlike the Corinthians, did not allow his rights and freedoms to distract him from making sure that everything in his life pointed to the real attraction, Jesus Christ. We are to follow Paul's lead.

Characteristic #2: They frequently and persuasively share the Good News of Jesus Christ.

Encouraged and empowered by the Spirit, every believer is to be in the business of gospel persuasion. We know that we are not the ones persuading unbelievers to God; God is persuading them through us.

Earlier, in 1 Corinthians 2:4–5, Paul laid out his evangelism strategy: "And my speech and my preaching were not with persuasive words of human wisdom, but in demonstration of the Spirit and of power, that your faith should not be in the wisdom of men but in the power of God" (NKJV). Paul didn't think that he was on his own rescuing people from hell. No, he persuaded people to the Lord through the Lord's power. He was merely a tool through which the Lord worked. Dawson Trotman, the founder of The Navigators, said, "Soul-winners are not soul-winners because of *what* they know, but *Who* they know, and how much they want others to know Him."[50]

We do not have the right to be silent about Jesus—His love, His cross, His mercy, and His offer of eternal life. Yet sadly, that's exactly what many are doing. The majority of church members will never lead a single person to saving faith in Jesus by sharing the gospel with him or her in a coherent, invitational way.

I don't mean to be judgmental here; I'm just trying to be direct. If you aren't taking advantage of regular opportunities to be a faithful witness of God's incredible salvation through His Son, Jesus, you are not living as a "whatever it takes" kind of Christian. You may be on the team, but you aren't in the game.

Maybe you think this is overly radical. Possibly, but so is the gospel. It's radical that God would come out of heaven, clothe Himself in human flesh, hang out with sinners, live a perfect life, and allow evil, depraved people to beat, mock, and crucify Him. It's radical that Jesus predicted before His death that He would rise again and prove His power over sin, death, and hell. It's radical that His plan to save the world involves people like you and me sharing His saving message everywhere we go, every chance we get. Yes, it's radical, but it doesn't lessen our responsibility.

We need to follow the example of Peter and John, who were imprisoned for sharing the Good News of Jesus and further threatened by the authorities to stop talking to others about Him. Do you know what their response was? They said, "As for us, we cannot help speaking about what we have seen and heard" (Acts 4:20). We, on the other hand, are often silent, even with no threat of pain or trouble in sight. Not even the threat of death could shut these men up. It only fueled their evangelistic fervor.

I tend to agree with Andrew Murray, who claimed that there are only two classes of Christians: soul-winners and backsliders.[51] In which camp do you currently find yourself? If we know the cure for sin, the source of joy, the hope of the world, and the only way to eternal life, then it is a serious offense against our gracious God to be silent saints. We need to hear these words echo in our minds: "Woe to me if I do not preach the gospel!" (1 Corinthians 9:16b).

Characteristic #3: They connect with culture without compromising their conduct.

Paul was not telling Christians to lay aside their biblical principles but to lay aside their personal preferences when working to advance the gospel:

> *To the Jews I became like a Jew, to win the Jews. To those under the law I became like one under the law (though I myself am not under the law), so as to win those under the law. To those not having the law I became like one not*

> ***having the law (though I am not free from God's law but am under Christ's law), so as to win those not having the law. To the weak I became weak, to win the weak.***
>
> ***—1 Corinthians 9:20–22a***

This doesn't mean that we should live like unbelievers to win unbelievers. We don't become like adulterers to win adulterers. No, Paul was not talking about adjusting right and wrong for others. We are never called to compromise truth.

There are two parts to Old Testament law: the moral law and the ceremonial law. The *moral law* applies to everyone for all time. Everyone everywhere is accountable for obeying this part of the law. It's impossible for us to obey the moral law, however, unless we have the Spirit of God living in us. That's why being good or trying hard doesn't cut it.

Our righteousness does not depend on our behavior or performance. Our righteousness depends on the finished work of Jesus Christ, applied to us by grace through faith. The Spirit then moves in and empowers us to obey the moral law of God.

Then, there is the *ceremonial law*, which applied to the nation of Israel. Some Jews—both Messianic and Orthodox—still observe many or most aspects of ceremonial law. These are laws that marked the people of God as a unique and separate people, but they are not binding for Gentile Christians today.

For example, you may have heard people say, "The Old Testament says homosexuality is wrong (Leviticus 18:22), but it also says that we shouldn't eat catfish and shrimp (Leviticus 11:9–12). So how can you say that one is wrong and the other is not?" Well, that's very clear. One has to do with the moral law of God for everyone for all time, and the other has to do with ceremonial purity laws for the nation of Israel and does not apply to Gentile

Christians (Acts 15).

The moral law is of the Old Testament, but it is also reinforced for us in the New Testament, while the ceremonial law is not. Paul essentially said that he would not disobey the moral law of God, but he was flexible with the ceremonial part. Following or not following any of those rules had no effect on his spiritual life. Yet, if following them would open a door for sharing the gospel with the Jews, he would gladly do so.

To the Jews, Paul became like a Jew. If they didn't eat pork, he didn't eat pork. If they went to the synagogue, he went to the synagogue. If they observed a certain type of ceremonial feast, Paul observed it. In doing so, he wasn't selling out to the culture; he was simply staying connected to it. In matters he did not consider ethically or theologically essential or implied by the gospel, Paul believed in flexibility. Because these things didn't corrupt his theology or compromise his character, he was willing to use them as opportunities to preach the gospel of Jesus Christ effectively and win unbelievers to the Lord.

For instance, when I travel to India with a mission team, we don't eat beef. Why? For the people's sake. They believe that cows are sacred, and if they saw us eating beef, they'd never be able to get past that to hear what we have to share with them. It's our joy and pleasure not to eat beef while we're there so that we don't create obstacles for the gospel. As soon as we get back to the United States, however, we have steak for dinner! Paul refused to let cultural practices hinder his mission to preach the gospel.

Here's another example that comes closer to where I live. Let's say your neighbors are Roman Catholic by name but don't personally know Jesus, and you're trying to share the gospel with them. You've built a relationship with them and started spending time together, and they invite you over for supper one night. Through your conversations, you know that they believe it's extremely inappropriate and disrespectful if you don't make the sign of the cross before and after you pray.

Now, you know that you don't have to make the sign of the cross to pray. It's something you could do as a reminder of Jesus' sacrifice, but you don't have to do it. You know that your access to God is through Jesus, not through any religious ritual. You know that you have every right not to make the sign of the cross.

However, out of love for that Roman Catholic family and your zealous desire for them to know Jesus, you will lay down your right and honor the people who are not under Christ's law. You will make the sign of the cross when they pray because you don't want to set up an obstacle to sharing the gospel with them. Your love will compel you to submit to their morally neutral religious ritual if it increases your chances of personally proclaiming the gospel of grace to them.

As Christians, we are called to build bridges and burn barriers. Many churches and Christians do just the opposite when it comes to reaching people who are far from God. They build barriers and burn bridges. Obviously, this doesn't help soften hearts or advance the gospel.

Characteristic #4: They modify their methods while maintaining the message.

Paul wrote:

> *I have become all things to all people so that by all possible means I might save some. I do all this for the sake of the gospel, that I may share in its blessings.*
>
> ***—1 Corinthians 9:22b–23***

It's easy for many in the church to have a consumer

mentality and fight any change that doesn't suit them. There are two things you are sure to find in every church you visit. First, people will resist change, not wanting to go outside of their comfort zone. Second, in seeming contradiction, people don't like how things currently are!

When members treat the church like their own country club, we shouldn't be surprised when outsiders have no desire to join. They don't want our preferences; they need God's promises. Anything not mandated by Scripture that we are unwilling to change for God's glory is likely an idol. But when our hearts burn for those far from God to know, love, and trust Him, the preferences that we are so quick to defend have a lesser pull on us.

British missionary C.T. Studd said, "Some want to live within the sound of a church or chapel bell; I want to run a rescue shop within a yard of hell."[52] In a very real way, that was Corinth. God, through Paul, planted a church within shouting distance of hell and began graciously rescuing Corinthians from their impending doom. Paul was willing to change anything in his lifestyle or approach to ministry if it meant greater success in reaching more people for Christ.

Paul understood that God has chosen to use people to reach people. He refused to sacrifice the message but was ready to sacrifice the messenger. He wasn't willing to change the message, but he was willing to change his methods. Paul was determined to live in such a way that everything he did was for the sake of the gospel, and his life shined because of it.

Pastor Erwin Lutzer told the story of gold found in a Montana riverbed in the 1850s.[53] This incredible treasure was discovered by a group of ten people. The problem was that their bodies were tired, their tools were broken, and their food supply was running low. They said to one another, "There's no way we can get all this gold out with the supplies we have, so let's go back to the closest town to get what we need. But let's promise each other that we won't tell anyone what we found. We'll get some rest, buy our supplies, and then come back to get all the gold for ourselves."

Ten days later, when they left the little town with their supplies to retrieve the gold, fifty of the townspeople followed them. They couldn't believe it! Each of them began to accuse the other: "I didn't tell anyone. Did you?" "I didn't say a word, did you?"

The townspeople revealed the source. They said, "We knew you had found gold by the smiles on your faces!" They couldn't hide what was inside.

Do the people around you know that you've found spiritual gold in Jesus Christ? Are you actively and eagerly sharing with them the priceless treasure of the gospel? If so, keep it up! If not, what's holding you back?

Do What Angels Cannot

Wouldn't it be much easier and far more effective if God used His angels as His gospel ambassadors to this lost world? After all, most humans in Scripture who encountered angels fell on their faces in sheer terror. The angels overwhelmed these mortals with their presence and power. That would surely get the attention of unbelievers and change their minds, right?

But God has chosen us, not angels. Why? Because angels have not experienced the life-changing power of the resurrection of Jesus. We have. No heavenly angel has been headed to hell under the wrath of God due to sin. We have. They have never had their hearts gripped so tightly by the convicting power of the Spirit that all they knew to do was throw themselves on the love and mercy of their Creator. We have.

No angel can sing with experiential fervor, "Amazing grace, how sweet the sound, that saved a wretch like me."[54] Why? Because they've never been wretches in need of being rescued. Ah, but we have! It is our duty to tell because it has been our delight to experience.

Would you stop and pray right now? Would you ask God for a generous outpouring of Jesus' "whatever it takes" attitude upon yourself and your local church in winning others through the good news of the gospel?

When Christians are busy working together to win the lost, we have little time, energy, or desire to focus on our own plans or fight over our preferences. We become unified in our indispensable mission of sharing Christ's gospel with the world.

WORKBOOK

Chapter Six Questions

Question: What words would best describe your desire to see lost souls come to Christ? Would words such as *passion*, *zeal*, *fire*, *obsession*, *determination*, or *sacrifice* correctly characterize your soul-winning attitude, or would words such as *apathy*, *fear*, *distraction*, and *secondary* be more accurate? What words do you want to describe your heart for evangelism?

Question: What are some rights that you have waived or may need to waive in order to reach the lost for Christ more effectively? Describe some sacrifices you have made to win souls for Christ.

____

____

____

____

____

____

____

____

____

____

____

____

Question: Describe the culture around your church and in the largest city near you. Are there subcultures of differing nationalities, socioeconomic classes, and religious backgrounds? What are some practical, real-life ways you can connect with each culture in your community without compromising your moral conduct?

____

____

____

____

____

____

____

____

____

____

____

____

Action: Evaluate your church's understanding of how to share the gospel. If you're a pastor, offer training in personal evangelism and discipleship as well as training in basic apologetics and how to engage the culture for Christ.

Chapter Six Notes

CHAPTER SEVEN

The Motive: Racing for a Reward

Do you not know that in a race all the runners run, but only one gets the prize? Run in such a way as to ***get the prize.***
—1 Corinthians 9:24 **(emphasis added)**

Some Christians want enough of Christ to be identified with Him but not enough to be seriously inconvenienced.[55]

—D.A. Carson

Have you ever heard of a marathon in which five-thousand people started the race, but only one runner finished the entire race and got the prize? It happened in May 2013 in Sunderland, England, in a race called the Marathon of the North. The unfortunate fiasco took place when the second- and third-place runners lost sight of the first-place runner, who was following the vehicle responsible for showing the correct route.

Incredibly, the second- and third-place runners took a wrong turn and led the other 4,997 contestants the wrong way. By the time the mistake was discovered, it was too late. Every runner except the leader ran 264 meters short of the 26.2 miles required for a marathon. As the contestants came across the finish line, they were informed that they had been disqualified from the race. Only the athlete who ran the full distance on the correct course received the prize.[56]

No Participation Trophies

Can you imagine how disappointing it would be to put in all that effort, toil, sweat, and pain to run all but 264 meters of a 26.2-mile race just to find out at the end that you were disqualified from receiving the prize? At the end of 1 Corinthians 9, the apostle Paul compared living the Christian life to running a race. His passionate charge to the Corinthians was to run this race to win it. We can infer from his challenge that losing is a real possibility. You can lose this race and its reward by being disqualified:

> *Do you not know that in a race all the runners run, but only one gets the prize? Run in such a way as to get the prize. ... No, I strike a blow to my body and make it my slave so that after I have preached to others, I myself will not be disqualified for the prize.*
>
> ***—1 Corinthians 9:24, 27***

The word *preach* in the original language, *kerusso*, means "to herald."[57] At the Isthmian Games, there was a man whose duty it was to serve as a public announcer. He was known as the herald, and he was responsible for several tasks. At the beginning of each event, he introduced the competitors to the crowd and outlined the rules to the contestants. Anyone violating the rules was disqualified. The herald also reminded everyone of the desired prize awaiting the winner.[58]

In this passage, Paul envisioned himself as both herald

and competitor. He admitted that it would be embarrassing to know all the rules of the race and explain them to others only to be disqualified from the ultimate prize because he didn't abide by the rules himself.

Paul was not fearful of losing eternal life with Christ. Salvation cannot be earned or lost by human effort or works; it is the free gift of God's grace. The same grace that saves us for Christ also secures us in Christ. Paul was talking about being disqualified from receiving eternal rewards.

Every born-again believer entered this spiritual race the moment he or she believed the gospel and was welcomed into God's family. This race is the passionate pursuit of internal holiness and the production of external fruitfulness—in other words, sanctification. We aim to become more and more like Christ internally so that we work better and better for Christ externally. Jesus qualified us for the race through His cross, but He rewards us for our race by how we choose to run. Heaven knows nothing of participation trophies.

Racing for a Reward

Paul suggested that the Corinthians were running a poor race, evidenced by the discord and division among them. They were in danger of being disqualified for any eternal rewards when they stood before Jesus in eternity. Paul presented two contrasting examples of how this all-important race of life can be run. One leads to reward; the other leads to disqualification. His challenge was meant to inspire the Corinthians to turn their eyes from the temporary to the eternal:

> *Everyone who competes in the games goes into strict training. They do it to get a crown that will not last, but we do*

it to get a crown that will last forever.
—1 Corinthians 9:25

The athletes participating in the Isthmian Games pushed themselves vigorously to gain a prestigious crown made of greenery. It was a high honor in the moment but faded over time. The athletes' names and accomplishments are long forgotten. However, the believer who wins the race of the Christian life will receive a crown from Jesus that will never fade or be forgotten.

Christians who don't live well aren't disqualified from God's family, but a life poorly lived isn't divinely celebrated. All those in heaven will be equally saved, but we won't be equally rewarded. God will honor those in heaven who honored Him on earth through a passionate pursuit of holiness and fruitfulness.

Paul, knowing that every believer can win the race and receive this crown, offered an expert strategy on how to run victoriously.

Tactic #1: Be killing the monster.

Paul was determined to discipline himself to run the best race possible. How? He wrote, "I strike a blow to my body and make it my slave" (1 Corinthians 9:27). Huh? Was Paul a masochist? Was he into self-flagellation and punishment? No. He was not talking about his physical body or flesh but his spiritual flesh. Old-time theologians called it "mortifying the flesh."

The *flesh* refers to that part of every person's heart that longs to be selfish, sinful, and rebellious. It's a hungry internal monster that constantly craves self-satisfaction. Feeding it will never satiate its appetite; it must be starved to death. Even after salvation, every Christ-follower still has a part of his or her heart that wars against God.

Paul specifically addressed this inner battle in his letter to the church in Colossae:

> *So put to death the sinful, earthly things lurking within you. Have nothing to do with sexual immorality, impurity, lust, and evil desires. Don't be greedy, for a greedy person is an idolater, worshiping the things of this world.*
>
> ***—Colossians 3:5** (NLT)*

That's the flesh that lurks within us. Paul was saying, "I constantly have to beat up that part of my heart that wants its own way and wants to be its own god. I will not let it own or control me. In God's strength, I will constantly discipline myself to master it." The truth is that either you will be a slave to your flesh or your flesh will be a slave to you. You will control your flesh, or your flesh will control you. There is no middle ground.

Tactic #2: Be centered on the gospel.

The power to defeat the flesh daily is not our own. It is the power of God given to us through the gospel of Jesus Christ. We don't graduate to greater things once we've been saved by the gospel—there is nothing greater than the gospel! The same gospel that saves us also strengthens and sustains us. It reminds us of Who is in us and for us.

But the gospel doesn't just redirect our eternal destiny; it should redefine every aspect of our earthly lives. Let me give a few examples.

1. Education: The purpose of your schoolwork is not just to make you smart. The purpose of your schoolwork is to sharpen your mind and refine your skills so you can understand the gospel more clearly and fully and communicate it more effectively. So, your education is about the gospel.

2. Vocation: The same goes for your job. Your job is not just about making money, having a career, or finding fulfillment in life. Your job is about the gospel. You work so that you can have a constant platform to live out and share the gospel. You are to build relationships with the people you work with who don't know the gospel, and you are to earn money to give to the mission of spreading the gospel to the ends of the earth. Your vocation is about the gospel.

3. Marriage: Likewise, your marriage is about the gospel. It's not just about companionship, children, and tax deductions. Your marriage is a picture of Jesus' union with the church (Ephesians 5). It is a teaching tool that God uses to display His love and grace through human relationships. The Good News of Jesus will likely make more sense to your neighbors if they see it in your life before they hear it from your lips. Your marriage is to be all about the gospel.

4. Family: Your family is also about the gospel. Your main concern for your children should not be what college they will attend or what kind of career they will need to be successful. Your primary concern for them should be that they love Jesus and pour out their lives for His glory and gospel. Who cares about raising athletes, scholars, doctors, or lawyers if they aren't in love with the Savior and Creator of the world? Our first mission field is our own family. Your family is about the gospel.

5. Church: Your local church, of course, is to be all about the gospel. You have vowed together to proclaim and display the radical love and grace of God found supremely in Jesus. Together, you're committed to practicing humility, patience, servanthood, and generosity. Likewise, you have given permission to hold each other accountable, with love, when the traits and characteristics of Jesus are not being properly demonstrated. You see, the church is full of fellow runners who aren't just focused on their own race but have promised to humbly serve and passionately support the believers who run alongside them.

Allowing the gospel to invade, transform, and shine out of every aspect of life fuels Christ-followers who are running the race of the Christian life with a desire to win.

Tactic #3: Be focused on the finish.

Paul wrote, "Everyone who competes in the games goes into strict training. They do it to get a crown that will not last, but we do it to get a crown *that will last forever*" (1 Corinthians 9:25, emphasis added). Paul never took his eyes off the finish line of life that leads immediately into forever. When you lose sight of how you want to finish, you lose the passion and forget the purpose for which you run.

During the 1968 Olympic games in Mexico City, a Tanzanian marathoner took a brutal fall. He was bloodied and badly hurt, but he exercised tremendous perseverance and courage and refused to quit. He finished so far behind the other runners that only a few spectators remained in the stadium to see it. A reporter asked him why he continued to run. The marathoner spoke these immortal words: "My country did not send me five thousand miles to start the race. They sent me to finish it."[59]

Jesus came much further and sacrificed far more to get us to the finish line of life in victorious fashion. Paul wrote the following words:

> *Not that I have already obtained all this, or have already arrived at my goal, but I press on to take hold of that for which Christ Jesus took hold of me. ... But one thing I do: Forgetting what is behind and straining toward what is ahead, I press on toward the goal to win the prize for*

> *which God has called me heavenward in Christ Jesus.*
> ***—Philippians 3:12–14***

You may just be starting your race, or you may be in the middle of your race, or you may be on the very last lap. Wherever you are, it's never too late to finish strong. Press on! Leave stuff behind! Forget about your start and get focused on the finish!

On his deathbed, the great evangelist D.L. Moody spoke these last words:[60]

> Earth recedes; heaven opens before me. ... If this is death, it is sweet! There is no valley here! God is calling me, and I must go! ... This is my triumph; this is my coronation day!

He knew that he had run his race well, and he was ready to receive his promised prize.

By describing his own tactics for winning the race, Paul was not trying to impress the Corinthians but to inspire them to turn their eyes away from themselves and focus on Jesus, who would be waiting at the finish line for them.

Racing to Be Disqualified

You see, it matters who we are. It matters how we live. It matters where we serve. It matters what our attitude is. It matters how well and how often we share the gospel. It matters because God says it matters.

The Corinthian Christians were being warned that they were headed toward disqualification. No doubt their minds were racing as they wondered how that was possible. What does a disqualified life look like? Paul anticipated this question and essentially said in the first half of 1 Corinthians 10, "Let me give you a sad example of people who ran poorly and missed out. Listen and learn from their mistakes."

Mistake #1: Overconfidence

The Israelites' overconfidence stemmed from the fact that they confused spiritual blessings with God's approval. More blessings from God do not make us more loved by God; they just make us more accountable to Him. God's abundant blessings are not meant to make us spiritually slower and fatter, hindering our race. One day, we will be held accountable for every blessing that was bestowed upon us.

Note all the blessings Israel had received:

> *For I do not want you to be ignorant of the fact, brothers and sisters, that our ancestors were all under the cloud [God's presence] and that they all passed through the sea [God's power]. They were all baptized into Moses [God's leadership] in the cloud and in the sea. They all ate the same spiritual food and drank the same spiritual drink [God's provision]; for they drank from the spiritual rock that accompanied them, and that rock was Christ [God's salvation].*
>
> ***—1 Corinthians 10:1–4** [comments added]*

The Israelites whom God led out of Egypt were all radically blessed, but nearly all of them were divinely disqualified: "Nevertheless, God was not pleased with most of them; their bodies were scattered in the wilderness" (1 Corinthians 10:5).

God littered the desert with the bodies of His people. Why? Because He didn't love them anymore? No. Because He changed His mind about them? No. Because He couldn't get the job done? No.

It was because they refused to run diligently and obediently the spiritual race He had set before them. They had been saved from Egypt by God's grace. They were never sent back to Egypt, but they didn't run the race with determination and discipline in the right direction. Their failure to run the race cost them everything. God disqualified them through death. Do you know where they are now? In heaven. Will they be rewarded for how they used and abused the blessings of God? No.

Paul was saying to the Corinthians and to us, "Don't think that because you've been incredibly blessed by God that you are free to live however you choose with those blessings. You are accountable. If you treat God's blessing the same way the Israelites did, you will be disqualified just as they were." Don't get so overconfident that you fail to remember that the same God who richly blessed you will also promptly disqualify you.

Mistake #2: Disobedience

Israel embraced evil desires over God's will. When God saves you, He eliminates any possibility of you having to pay the penalty for your sin. Christ did that for you on the cross. However, while the penalty for sin has been eliminated, all the consequences of sin have not.

One potential consequence of ongoing, unrepentant sin is disqualification. You would think that the Israelites would have said to God, "You have done so much for us, Lord. We are Yours completely. Do with us what You will." Right? But they didn't. Paul wrote:

> *Now these things occurred as examples to keep us from setting our hearts on evil things as they did.*
>
> ***—1 Corinthians 10:6***

This is a wake-up call! If our sins correspond with their sins, then our judgment will correspond with their judgment. What were the sins that led to their disqualification?

- *Idolatry:* "Do not be idolaters, as some of them were; as it is written: 'The people sat down to eat and drink and got up to indulge in revelry'" (1 Corinthians 10:7).
- *Immorality:* "We should not commit sexual immorality, as some of them did—and in one day twenty-three thousand of them died" (1 Corinthians 10:8).
- *Immaturity:* "We should not test Christ, as some of them did—and were killed by snakes" (1 Corinthians 10:9).
- *Ingratitude:* "And do not grumble, as some of them did—and were killed by the destroying angel" (1 Corinthians 10:10).

We all likely recognize the severity of the first three areas of sin. But what about that last one? Grumbling is complaining. It's griping and murmuring. It's expressing unwarranted dissatisfaction. It's complaining about what God is doing or where God has placed you. It's complaining that you don't have what you want or that others have more.

The Israelites had been given so much, yet they complained that it wasn't enough. "It's not enough that You rescued us from slavery. It's not enough that You dropped food from the sky and caused water to gush from a rock. It's not enough that You are with us all the time. It's not enough that You promise to take us to a land flowing with milk and honey. It's not enough for You to be our God and for us to be Your people. It's not enough. We want more!"

As American Christians, we complain so much that you'd think it was our God-given spiritual gift. And boy do we use it! What do you find yourself grumbling about these days? Complaining words are evidence of an ungrateful heart. Your heart is essentially crying out to God, "The cross is not enough. Your Spirit within me is not enough. Your Word is not enough. The job You have provided for me is not enough. This spouse beside me is not enough. This house is not enough. This family is not enough. This church is not enough. This life I have is not enough. I want more. I deserve more. God, stop doing what You are doing and do what I want You to do!"

Do you think that you can rail against Him who has given you all things and everything will be just fine? I don't think so. Ingratitude isn't just a little quirk. It's a disqualifier. An ungrateful heart revealed by a complaining tongue forfeits eternal rewards.

Mistake #3: Independence

All three of our children went through a phase as toddlers when they didn't want Mom or Dad to help them with anything. They would sternly say, "I do it myself!" The Israelites were acting like toddlers by refusing God's help to defeat temptation, which in turn led them away from total dependence and obedience.

> *These things happened to them as examples and were written down as warnings for us, on whom the culmination of the ages has come. So, if you think you are standing firm, be careful that you don't fall! No temptation has overtaken you except what is common to mankind. And God is faithful; he will not let you be tempted beyond what you can bear. But when you are tempted, he will also provide a way*

out so that you can endure it.

—1 Corinthians 10:11–13

God knows what will grow you and what will break you. He controls the size of your temptation from Satan and provides an escape route. Often the temptation is self-centered, so the escape is the opportunity to help someone else who is suffering or struggling. Temptation loses its grip on us when we stop giving it all of our attention. Our independence leads to insulation and isolation. These are permanent fixtures of the devil's playground.

The temptation to pull away and run the race by ourselves is common to us all. However, you have an extraordinary God, who will always provide you with another way to go, run, and succeed. You don't have to fail. You don't have to run alone. You don't have to succumb to temptation. It's your choice. The temptation to stir dissension or remain divided is strong, and it's straight from the devil himself. God's way of escape often leads straight to the door of those you're fighting or avoiding.

In the 1988 Winter Olympics, American speed skater Dan Jansen was favored to win a gold medal. The day before his first race, Dan received word that his sister had died following a long bout with leukemia. Bearing the weight of his sorrow, he laced on his skates to win for his sister. On the first turn, he lost his balance and fell, causing him to lose the race. Four days later, in the 1,000-meter race, he fell again.

The whole country mourned over Dan Jansen's failures. According to *Sports Illustrated*, Dan received countless letters of compassionate consolation.[61] One letter among them was remarkable. It was from Mark Arrowood, a thirty-year-old man from Doylestown, Pennsylvania, with mental disabilities.

Mark wrote:

> Dear Dan, I watched you on TV. I'm sorry that you fell two times. I am in Special Olympics. I won a gold medal at Pa. State Summer Olympics right after my Dad died seven years ago. ... Before we start the games we have a saying that goes like this. "Let me win but if I can't win let me be brave in the attempt." ... I want to share one of my gold medals with you because I don't like to see you not get one. Try again in four more years.

Inside the envelope, Dan found the gold medal Mark won in a track-and-field event. Through the care and concern of a fellow competitor, Dan realized that he might have lost, but he wasn't defeated. And he wasn't alone. Against all odds, he went on to win his first and only Olympic gold medal six years later.

Christian, you alone must run your race, but you must not run your race alone. You will not win by yourself. In the Lord's strength, resist the temptations that lead to disqualification. Then you will experience your reward, and you will never regret giving your life to receive it.

WORKBOOK

Chapter Seven Questions

Question: At the end of 1 Corinthians 9, Paul compared the Christian life to a race. Taking an honest look at your own life, how would you say you are doing in this spiritual race? Are you becoming more holy inwardly and bearing fruit outwardly? Give some concrete examples of ways you've grown or born fruit recently.

____

____

____

____

____

____

____

____

____

____

Question: According to this chapter, overconfidence, disobedience, and independence can hold individuals back in the spiritual race of the Christian life. Which of these three areas is most difficult for you? What efforts can you make to change in that area?

____

____

____

____

____

____

____

____

____

____

____

____

Question: As a Christian, you do not have to run your race alone. How can you rely on the Holy Spirit to help you succeed? Give examples of times when you were facing a decision and He guided you and helped you to resist temptation.

____

____

____

____

____

____

____

____

____

____

____

____

Action: This chapter suggests that every believer can win his or her race and provides a strategy for success. List the tactics mentioned in the chapter and brainstorm how you can increase your chances to succeed in each area. Write down concrete changes you can make to ensure that you will win your race. Think of ways you can create accountability for yourself.

Chapter Seven Notes

CONCLUSION

The Goal: All for the Glory of God

So whether you eat or drink or whatever you do, do it all for the glory of God.

—1 Corinthians 10:31

...the will of God for your life is pretty straightforward: Be holy like Jesus, by the power of the Spirit, for the glory of God.[62]

—Kevin DeYoung

Sometimes life doesn't go the way we think it should. I heard a story about a man who was working on his motorcycle on the patio outside his house. He accidentally knocked the motorcycle into gear, and as he held on to the handlebars, it dragged him through the glass patio door into the dining room.

His wife, hearing the crash, ran into the dining room and found her husband lying on the floor, cut and bleeding, with the motorcycle lying next to him and the patio door shattered. She grabbed her phone and called for an ambulance. After the ambulance arrived and took the man to the hospital, his wife stood the motorcycle up and rolled it outside. She noticed that some gasoline had spilled on the dining room floor, so she wiped it up with some paper towels and threw them into the toilet.

The husband was treated at the hospital and then released to come home. When he arrived, he surveyed the shattered patio door and the damage done to his motorcycle. It depressed him so much that he went into the bathroom and sat down on the toilet to smoke a cigarette. Once he finished the cigarette, he dropped it between his legs into the toilet bowl.

The wife heard a loud explosion and her husband screaming. She ran into the bathroom and found her husband lying on the floor. His pants had been blown off, and he had suffered burns to the "sitting area" of his body.

The wife again quickly called for an ambulance. The same ambulance crew came and loaded the husband onto a stretcher for the second time that day. As they were going down the stairs, one of the paramedics asked the wife how her husband burned himself. As she told them the story, the paramedics started laughing so hard that they tilted the stretcher sideways and dumped the husband off. He fell down the remaining stairs and broke his ankle.

Live for the Ultimate Goal

Sometimes life just doesn't go the way we think it should. And when it's your own story, it's not nearly so humorous. Paul's life was full of events that could have led him to question God's love for him or God's control over the details of his life.

Jesus called Paul to be a missionary, taking the gospel all over the world. And for nearly twenty-five years, that's precisely what he did. He went on three different missionary journeys and started churches all over Asia and

Europe. He preached the gospel in Damascus, Syria, Cyprus, Pisidian Antioch, Iconium, Lystra, Derbe, Jerusalem, Philippi, Thessalonica, Berea, Athens, Corinth, and Ephesus.

What happened to Paul as a result of his diligent obedience to Jesus? In several of those cities, people started riots and tried to kill Paul for preaching the gospel. He was physically forced out of Damascus, Iconium, Thessalonica, Berea, Ephesus, and Jerusalem. He was beaten and thrown in jail in Philippi. He received thirty-nine lashes from the Jews on five different occasions, and three times he was beaten with rods. Once he was stoned by Jews and left for dead outside the city.

Why would Paul continue this mission that constantly led him into personal pain and turmoil? We've already answered this question, haven't we? Because he had experienced the life-transforming, eternity-changing power of Jesus found only in the gospel. He was called by God and compelled by His love to deliver this good news to everyone everywhere, no matter the personal cost. He knew that the race of the Christian life was tough, but he was confident that Jesus would meet him at the finish line and rejoice with him forever.

At the very end of his three-chapter argument to the Corinthian church, Paul adamantly highlighted the ultimate goal for his life, ministry, and mission:

> *"I have the right to do anything," you say—but not everything is beneficial. "I have the right to do anything"—but not everything is constructive. ... So whether you eat or drink or whatever you do, do it all for the glory of God.*
>
> ***—1 Corinthians 10:23, 31*** ***(emphasis added)***

It's as if Paul could hear the Corinthians asking why they should sacrifice personal freedoms and liberties for the sake of others who might not accept or appreciate it. Paul finished his argument by underscoring what all Christ-followers should be aiming for in every decision we make and every action we take. Everything we think, do, say, give, and give up—all the way down to the basics of eating and drinking—should be for the fulfillment of one supreme goal: to bring glory to our great God. But how do we do that?

1. Ask the question constantly.

If we can glorify God in *whatever we do*, then we had better ask this question before we do anything: *Does it glorify God?* This action or activity may not be biblically prohibited, but it still might not be spiritually beneficial. It could be a freedom you have the right to exercise, but it may be of little help to the bride of Christ. Those are good reasons to limit your liberties and sacrifice your freedoms.

Paul, however, took it one step further. He was saying, "Put yourself and other believers to the side for a moment. Forget how eating meat or not eating meat affects you or other believers. Just ask this one simple question of everything you do in life: Does this glorify your God?"

2. Understand the meaning correctly.

It's easy to say that we desire God's glory without understanding what this actually means. The psalmist said, "Glorify the LORD with me; let us exalt his name together" (Psalm 34:3).

What does it mean to glorify God? The Hebrew word translated as "glorify," *gadol*, can also be translated as "magnify" or "grow." It contains within it the idea of increasing the size of something.[63] In this context, it means to worship God for who He is and honor Him for what He has done. It is not God's radiant glory that is increasing so much as our ability to reflect God's glory to the world.

To glorify God means to feel, think, and act in ways that show off His greatness, majesty, splendor, and beauty. It means to make much of Him personally, privately, and publicly because He is worthy of our supreme devotion and dedication. We can and should do this in every aspect of our lives, whether major or mundane.

You see, our problem is that we think we bring God glory only when we do things like read the Bible, pray, go to church, share the gospel, feed the homeless, and sing old hymns. But Paul clearly explained that we have the ability to glorify God with *everything* we have and do in this life.

In other words, we can glorify God in our myriad daily activities, like driving to work, cleaning the bathroom, changing diapers, cooking supper, lying in a hospital bed, cheering at a game, dining with friends, taking a test, fixing a car, talking on the phone, going for a walk, solving a problem, or riding a wave. You see, it's not as much about the action we do as the attitude we have while we do it.

We can also glorify God and make much of Him by not doing things that we have the freedom to do, if abstaining from these things means that we are being more loving, generous, gracious, humble, sacrificial, selfless, or conscientious of others. The more we live and love like God the Son, the more glory we bring to God the Father. The ultimate question isn't whether something is right or wrong, if more people are for it or against it, or how many people will join or leave our church because of it. The question is whether we desire to bring maximum glory to our God through every detail of our lives.

I can't help but think that John Piper's famous quote has a flavor of this in mind: "God is most glorified in us when we are most satisfied in Him."[64]

3. Apply the principle personally.

The Corinthians were to eat meat or not eat meat for the glory of God above everything else. Seems easy enough, right? But what about us right now? How, for example, can we put up with screaming guitars and pounding drums in our church services when we prefer calmer, more serene worship? We glorify God by putting the preferences of others above our own and gratefully praise God for all of the people around us who are deeply engaged in connecting with the gracious God who saved us all.

How do we humble ourselves again and again to those around us who don't show the same courtesy or respect? We glorify God by having a greater desire to be like Jesus than to be right or feel superior.

How do we remain in rather than abandon the whiny small group that never seems to grow up or get past the basics? We glorify God by making it our joy to serve, love, teach, and encourage them every time we meet, thanking God for the growth He has given to us.

How do we keep sharing the gospel every opportunity we get with people who have shown no inclination to listen or believe? We glorify God by remembering that it's our privilege and purpose to proclaim the Good News, and it's His job to save them and change their hearts.

I could list a thousand everyday scenarios in which we can choose between what pleases us best and what glorifies God most. Every day we make countless decisions that reveal our hearts' desires and ultimate goals. Am I driven by a desire to make my life better for me so that I can enjoy it more or by a desire for God's glory to shine brighter so that the world can see and believe? David Platt said it best: "We go wherever God leads whenever God moves us … because we love His glory more than we love our lives."[65]

4. Cherish God's grace passionately.

How can we ever live like this consistently? Maybe I can last a day or two, but for the rest of my life? Come on, Paul! Give me a break! Well, Paul might not give you a break, but he will throw you a rescue rope. You might even call it your "rope of hope." It takes us right back to where Paul began his letter to these struggling saints: "I always thank my God for you because of *his grace* given you in Christ Jesus" (1 Corinthians 1:4, emphasis added).

How can we consistently keep God's glory as our ultimate goal? Only by God's amazing grace. Paul understood that the sole reason obedience and unity could be expected of the Corinthians was that they had experienced God's grace. We see God's glory only because of His grace, and it is only by His grace that we can live for His glory.

Grace Receivers and Deliverers

Several years ago, God gave me a front-row seat to the grandeur of His grace and glory that I will cherish for the rest of my days. I was on my first mission trip to India. Though I had done extensive research to prepare, "overwhelmed" would not even begin to describe how I felt in my foreign surroundings. My colleagues and I were there for a couple of weeks, equipping and encouraging local church pastors. They were some of the most humble and hospitable people I have ever met. Their tear-filled expressions of gratitude for our service to them were mind-blowing. I quickly realized, however, that God had sent me to India to learn more than to teach.

I'll never forget sitting in a chair while dozens of men, women, boys, and girls sat on a dirt floor singing praises to God at the top of their lungs for His wonderful kindness to them. Dozens more were lined up outside, straining to see and hear what was going on inside, wishing that there was room for more people to come inside.

Those inside didn't complain about the 120-degree heat, having to sit crowded together on a dirt floor, or having to sing a cappella. They were thrilled to worship their God and hear His Word from all five of their guest preachers from the United States. It was incredible, to say the least.

My fondest memory of the trip was when God set me up for an unforgettable lesson about His grace. Prior to leaving for India, I had bought several new shirts and pairs of pants made of a light material that could "breathe" in the country's hot, baking sun. A week into our trip, I needed to do some laundry. I was told by our hotel manager about a local launderer who would gladly clean, press, and fold all of my clothes for literally pennies on the dollar. For this frugal midwestern pastor, that sounded fantastic.

Sure enough, the next morning, all of my clothes were clean and neatly placed outside the door of our hotel room. It was a beautiful sight. Until I noticed *it*—a hole the size of a quarter in the knee of one of my pairs of pants! My fancy, lightweight, seventy-five-dollar pair of pants that I had worn only once! Just in case you can't tell, I was not at all pleased.

I called the hotel manager, and he came up to our room. I voiced my displeasure about the hole and even more about the fact that those responsible for the hole didn't mention it. Did they really think that I wouldn't notice? Did they think that I wouldn't care? Did they think that it was no big deal? Well, they thought wrong! I wanted an explanation. I wanted compensation. I wanted justice!

The manager patiently listened to my pitiful, entitled rant. He quickly got on the phone with the guilty party and had an impassioned conversation with him in a language I couldn't understand.

Finally, he hung up the phone and said, "Sir, you have a meeting with him tomorrow morning at eight o'clock. According to our local laws, you have the right to do with him what you want. You can require him to reimburse you for the pants or go to jail until he does."

But he wasn't done unloading his bombshell. "You probably need to know an important piece of information about the man you will meet. His salary is less than five dollars *a month*. He makes enough to feed his family, but it will be impossible for him to repay you. He is very sorry and very scared. He doesn't know what you will do with him, but he will be here first thing tomorrow morning to face you."

I don't think I slept that night. My soul was in agony. All I could do was tearfully ask God to forgive my pettiness and ignorance. What a fool I had been! The next day, I and a few other pastors went down to the small hotel lobby. When the local launderer saw me, he burst into tears as he threw himself at my feet, begging for mercy. With my broken heart beating out of my chest, I quickly picked him up and set him on his feet and hugged him as hard as I could. He stood there, stunned.

I slowly told him through an interpreter that I forgave him for his "crime" against me. I apologized for causing him such emotional and mental anguish. I promised not to hold this against him and made it clear that I did not require any form of reimbursement. Once again, after hearing this good news, he burst into tears, wanting to kiss my feet. I caught him on the way down and lifted him back up.

I wanted to show him more. That's when I said, "Sir, we are here in India sharing the Good News of Jesus, who is full of far greater kindness than I could ever show. Because of His mercy, He died in my place to take my pain and penalty for all of my sin against Him. Because of His perfect sacrifice, I've been forgiven by God fully and forever. I deserved punishment, but He has given me peace. Today, I pray that you will see His mercy through me."

Then I pulled a twenty-dollar bill from my pocket. "But my God is not just full of mercy; He is also full of grace. In His mercy, He doesn't give me what I deserve, which is punishment and hell. In His grace, He gives me what I don't deserve, like life, love, hope, joy, and eternity with Him."

I put the twenty-dollar bill in his hand. "I want to show you mercy by forgiving your debt. But even more, I want to show you grace by giving you more than you expect or deserve. Whenever you think of me and this moment, I want you to remember that this is all about Jesus and the goodness of the mercy and grace that He offers you."

God has called grace receivers to be grace deliverers. As Paul Tripp wisely shared, "It's not our weakness that limits the work of God in our life; it's the delusion of our own strength."[66] It was through my weakness that God's strength beamed brightly. We will never realize how unified we can be as a church until we admit how weak we truly are.

Unity is weak and will never last apart from a deep awareness of what Christ has done on our behalf. When His grace takes hold of us, however, we discover a power and motive for unity that can only be described as supernatural. Can you taste His grace? Are you ready to see what He might do through a church undivided? Let's build it together.

May these words encourage you as you build: "My grace is sufficient for you, for My strength is made perfect in weakness" (2 Corinthians 12:9 NKJV).

About the Author

Bob Ingle is the lead pastor of Waypoint Church, a multi-site church with locations in St. Charles and Wildwood, MO. For more than twenty-five years, he has successfully led churches through massive growth, necessary change, and the inevitable conflict that comes with both. Bob is widely known for his energy, insight, and humor in the preaching of God's Word. He loves helping people understand the timeless truths of Scripture and how to apply them to everyday life.

Bob earned his Master of Divinity degree in 1995 from Midwestern Baptist Theological Seminary in Kansas

City, MO. He is married to Jana, and they have three adult children: Adam, Avery, and Emma. Bob loves fishing, golfing, and rooting for his beloved Chicago Cubs, despite living in the heart of Cardinal Nation. Baseball is often discussed and debated but not allowed to bring division!

About Sermon To Book

SermonToBook.com began with a simple belief: that sermons should be touching lives, *not* collecting dust. That's why we turn sermons into high-quality books that are accessible to people all over the globe.

Turning your sermon series into a book exposes more people to God's Word, better equips you for counseling, accelerates future sermon prep, adds credibility to your ministry, and even helps make ends meet during tight times.

John 21:25 tells us that the world itself couldn't contain the books that would be written about the work of Jesus Christ. Our mission is to try anyway. Because in heaven, there will no longer be a need for sermons or books. Our time is now.

If God so leads you, we'd love to work with you on your sermon or sermon series.

Visit www.sermontobook.com to learn more.

REFERENCES

Notes

[1] Havner, Vance. *The Best of Vance Havner*. Baker Publishing Group, 1988, p. 91.

[2] Smith, Darin. "6 Marks of Gospel-Centered Unity." For the Church. September 14, 2017. https://ftc.co/resource-library/blog-entries/6-marks-of-gospel-centered-unity.

[3] "8:1–11:1." *ESV Study Bible*. Crossway, 2016, p. 2202.

[4] Faucett, Andrew. "Corinth." *Faucett's Bible Dictionary*. 1878. In Bible History Online. https://www.bible-history.com/faussets/c/corinth/.

[5] Strong, James. "G1577: ekklesia." *A Concise Dictionary of the Words in the Greek Testament and the Hebrew Bible*. Faithlife, 2019.

[6] Thielman, Frank S. "1 Corinthians: Timeline." *ESV Study Bible*. Crossway, 2008, p. 2188.

[7] Tripp, Paul D. "Walk with Unity." Wednesday Word Devotional. July 2, 2014. https://www.paultripp.com/wednesdays-word/posts/walk-with-unity.

[8] Keller, Timothy. *The Reason for God: Belief in an Age of Skepticism*. Penguin Publishing Group, 2008, p. 53-54.

[9] Jones, Steve. "Imitate God's Love." Sermon Search. https://www.sermonsearch.com/sermon-outlines/18745/imitate-gods-love-5-of-8/.

[10] "Kiss." *The Century Dictionary: An Encyclopedic Lexicon of the English Language, Part 3.* Edited by William Dwight Whitney. Century Company, 1889, p. 3294.

[11] DeYoung, Kevin. "Our Fellowship." University Reformed Church. January 23, 2015. Youtube. https://www.youtube.com/watch?v=Fy75JQQxgto.

[12] Lloyd-Jones, David Martin. *Christian Unity: An Exposition of Ephesians 4:1-10*. Baker, 1980, p. 41.

[13] Colson, Charles and Ellen Santilli Vaughn. *The Body*. Thomas Nelson, 1996, p. 82.

[14] Swindoll, Charles. *Insights on 1 & 2 Corinthians.* Tyndale House, 2017, p. 27.

[15] Strong, James. "G2675: katartizo." *A Concise Dictionary of the Words in the Greek Testament and the Hebrew Bible.* Faithlife, 2019.

[16] DeYoung, Kevin. "Kevin DeYoung." Twitter post, March 6, 2015, 9:25 a.m. https://twitter.com/RevKevDeYoung/status/573897179649216512.

[17] Sproul, R. C. *Everyone's a Theologian: An Introduction to Systematic Theology*. Reformation Trust, 2014, p. 12.

[18] Kopmeyer, M. R. *Thoughts to Build On.* UBS Publishers' Distributors, 2003.

[19] Welch, Edward T. *What Do You Think of Me? Why Do I Care?* New Growth Press, 2011, p. 117.

[20] Davey, Stephen. "A Recipe for Joy: To the Citizens of Heaven, Part 5." Wisdom for the Heart. October 5, 2014. https://www.twr360.org/mediahit/id,6117375/url,aHR0cHM6Ly8xMmE0ZWY3OTkzMmI0YWEyMTExZi01YzZiNjk5MmJhNDQxMTM4MGNmNGI3NjliYTA4YzQ2ZC5zc2wuY2YyLnJhY2tjZG4uY29tLzg2ODEwNC5wZGY_c2l0ZT10d3Iz NjA~.

---

[21] Thielman, Frank S. "8:1–11:1." *ESV Study Bible*. Crossway, 2016, p. 2202.

[22] Cowper, William. "Book iv." In *The Task*. Joseph Johnson, 1785.

[23] Welch, Ed. "Help from Someone Who Has Been There." Christian Counseling & Education Foundation. October 23, 2013. https://www.ccef.org/help-someone-who-has-been-there/.

[24] DeYoung, Kevin. *The Hole In Our Holiness: Filling the Gap Between Gospel Passion and the Pursuit of Godliness.* Crossway, 2014, p. 132.

[25] "Roethlisberger in 2005: '…The Safest Rider I Can Be.'" ESPN. June 12, 2006. https://www.espn.com/nfl/news/story?id=2481004.

[26] Branch, John. "Roethlisberger Is Seriously Injured in Motorcycle Wreck." *The New York Times*. June 13, 2006. https://www.nytimes.com/2006/06/13/sports/football/13steelers.html.

[27] "Big Ben Apologizes, Pledges He'll Ride Wearing Helmet." ESPN. June 14, 2016. https://www.espn.com/nfl/news/story?id=2484472.

[28] Fleming, David. "Life in the Fast Lane." ESPN. July 3, 2006. https://www.espn.com/espnmag/story?id=3662279.

[29] Platt, David. *Radical: Taking Back Your Faith from the American Dream.* Crown Publishing Group, 2010, p. 7.

[30] Elliot, Jim. In Elisabeth Elliot, *Shadow of the Almighty: The Life and Testament of Jim Elliot.* HarperCollins, 1989, p. 108.

[31] Swindoll, Charles and Bill Watkins. *Growing Up in God's Family: Bible Study Guide.* Insight for Living, 1986.

[32] Pentz, Victor D. "Left-Handed Power." Peachtree Presbyterian Church. December 15, 2013. http://peachtreechurch.org/Uploads/Messages/Transcripts/20131215sermon.pdf.

[33] See "Spurgeon's Love of Fine Cigars," The Spurgeon Archive. http://www.romans45.org/spurgeon/misc/cigars.htm.

[34] Wright, N. T. *Surprised by Hope: Rethinking Heaven, the Resurrection, and the Mission of the Church*. HarperOne, 2008, p. 144.

[35] Jacobs, Wayne. "Rights and Responsibilities." Ministry Lessons. June 3, 2018. https://waynejacobsministrylessons.wordpress.com/2018/06/03/rights-and-responsibilites/.

[36] Piper, John. In "John Piper Quotes." Twitter post, July 16, 2016. 6:33 p.m. https://twitter.com/JohnPiperDaily/status/754489074531069953.

[37] Snowden, Rita. In William Barclay, *The Letters to the Galatians and Ephesians*. Westminster John Knox Press, 1958, p. 133.

[38] Stetzer, Ed. "Bivocational Ministry as an Evagelism Opportunity." *The Exchange with Ed Stetzer*. Christianity Today. October 15, 2017. https://www.christianitytoday.com/edstetzer/2017/september/bivocational-ministry-as-evangelism-opportunity.html.

[39] Strong, James. "G1464: enkope." *A Concise Dictionary of the Words in the Greek Testament and the Hebrew Bible*. Faithlife, 2019.

[40] Strong, James. "G1465: egkopto." *A Concise Dictionary of the Words in the Greek Testament and the Hebrew Bible*. Faithlife, 2019.

[41] Sproul, R. C. Quoted in Bob Ditmer, "R.C. Sproul: Defender of the Evangelical Faith." Church Leaders. December 19, 2017. https://churchleaders.com/news/315330-r-c-sproul-defender-evangelical-faith.html.

[42] Chambers, Oswald. "Decreasing for His Purposes." In *My Utmost for His Highest*. Quoted in My Utmost for His Highest. March 24, 2019. https://utmost.org/decreasing-for-his-purpose/.

[43] Mohler, Albert. "Shepherds' Conference 2018, Dr. Albert Mohler Jr. (General Session 4)." July 1, 2018. Youtube. https://www.youtube.com/watch?v=dnH0DvRA0N8.

[44] Schwartz, Nick. "Will Smith Has a Hilarious Story About How Insanely Competitive Michael Jordan Is." *For the Win!* USA Today. December 15, 2017. https://ftw.usatoday.com/2017/12/will-smith-michael-jordan-competitive-jimmy-kimmel-story.

[45] Manfred, Tony and Scott Davis. "21 Examples of Michael Jordan's Insane Competitiveness." Business Insider. May 15, 2018. https://www.businessinsider.my/michael-jordans-insane-competitiveness-2014-7/.

[46] "Shaq Weighs In on Phil Jackson, Michael Jordan's Trash Talk and Les Miles." The Dan Patrick Show. November 28, 2012. http://www.danpatrick.com/2012/11/28/shaq-weighs-in-on-phil-jackson-michael-jordans-trash-talk-and-les-miles/.

[47] Newport, John Paul. "Bill Clinton Talks About His Game." *The Wall Street Journal.* October 15, 2011. https://www.wsj.com/articles/SB10001424052970204002304576631130160903012.

[48] Simmons, Bill. "Gambling and the Alpha Dog." ESPN The Magazine. June 19, 2006. http://www.espn.com/espn/page2/story?page=simmons/060614.

[49] "Imitate." Merriam-Webster. https://www.merriam-webster.com/dictionary/imitate.

[50] Moyer, R. Larry and Evan Tell. *31 Days with the Master Fisherman: A Daily Devotional on Bringing Christ to Others*. Kregel, 1997, p. 36.

[51] Rogers, Adrian. *What Every Christian Ought to Know*. Broadman & Homan Publishers, 2012, p. 86.

[52] Grubb, Norman. *C.T. Studd.* Christian Literature Crusade, 1972, p. 166.

[53] Lutzer, Erwin. *Coming to Grips with Your Role in the Workplace*. Moody Publishers, 1992.

[54] Newton, John. "Amazing Grace (How Sweet the Sound." 1779. In Hymnary.org. https://hymnary.org/text/amazing_grace_how_sweet_the_sound.

[55] Carson, D. A. *A Call to Spiritual Reformation: Priorities from Paul and His Prayers*. Inter-Varsity Press, 2011, p. 121.

[56] Smyth, Sara. "Bungling Marathon of the North Organisers Send 5,000 Runners the Wrong Way: Only the Eventual Winner Completed the Correct Course." The Daily Mail. May 16, 2013. https://www.dailymail.co.uk/news/article-2322966/5-000-Marathon-North-runners-didnt-complete-course-given-wrong-directions.html.

[57] Strong, James. "G2784: kerusso." *A Concise Dictionary of the Words in the Greek Testament and the Hebrew Bible.* Faithlife, 2019.

[58] Knox, Charles Eugene. "Thirty Eighth Sunday: The Games at the Isthmus." *A Year with St. Paul, or, Fifty-two Lessons for the Sundays of the Year*. A.D.F. Randolf, 1864, p. 242–249.

[59] "Marathon Man Akhwari Demonstrates Superhuman Spirit." Olympic.org. October 19, 1968. https://www.olympic.org/news/marathon-man-akhwari-demonstrates-superhuman-spirit.

[60] Moody, Paul Dwight and Arthur Percy Fitt. *The Shorter Life of D.L. Moody, Vol. 1: His Life*. The Bible Institute Colportage Association, 1900, p. 112.

[61] Wulf, Steve. "Scorecard." *Sports Illustrated.* June 27, 1988. https://www.si.com/vault/1988/06/27/106779225/scorecard.

[62] DeYoung, Kevin. *Just Do Something: A Liberating Approach to Finding God's Will.* Moody Publishers, 2014, p. 60.

[63] Strong, James. "H1431: gadal." *A Concise Dictionary of the Words in the Greek Testament and the Hebrew Bible.* Faithlife, 2019.

[64] Piper, John. "God Is Most Glorified in Us When We Are Most Satisfied in Him." Desiring God. October 13, 2012.

---

https://www.desiringgod.org/messages/god-is-most-glorified-in-us-when-we-are-most-satisfied-in-him.

[65] Platt, David. "Secret Church." Facebook post, September 15, 2014. https://www.facebook.com/secretchurch/posts/10152772895991204.

[66] Tripp, Paul. "Flee from Delusions of Strength." Desiring God. June 23, 2015. https://www.desiringgod.org/interviews/flee-from-delusions-of-strength.

Made in the USA
Monee, IL
04 March 2020